AMERICAN
WAR LIBRARY

★ The Cold War ★

Weapons of Peace: The Nuclear Arms Race

by Craig E. Blohm

AMERICAN
WAR LIBRARY

★ The Cold War ★

Weapons of Peace: The Nuclear Arms Race

by Craig E. Blohm

AMERICAN
WAR LIBRARY

⭐ The Cold War ⭐

Weapons of Peace: The Nuclear Arms Race

by Craig E. Blohm

LUCENT
BOOKS®

THOMSON
━━━━✶━━━━ ™
GALE

For more information, contact
Lucent Books
27500 Drake Rd.
Farmington Hills, MI 48331-3535
Or you can visit our Internet site at http://www.gale.com

LIBRARY OF CONGRESS CATALOGING-IN-PUBLICATION DATA

Blohm, Craig E., 1948–
    Weapons of peace : the nuclear arms race / by Craig E. Blohm.
        p. cm. — (American war library. The Cold War series)
Summary: Discusses the development of nuclear weapons, the race for nuclear
supremacy, deployment of these weapons during the Cold War, and disarmament.
Includes bibliographical references and index.
        ISBN 1-59018-212-X (hardback : alk. paper)
    1. Nuclear weapons—Juvenile literature.   2. Arms race—Juvenile literature.
3. Nuclear arms control—Juvenile literature.   4. World politics—1945—Juvenile
literature.   [1. Nuclear weapons.   2. Arms race.   3. Nuclear arms control.
4. World politics—1945–]   I. Title.
    U264 .B54 2003
    327.1'747—dc21   2002011035

Printed in the United States of America

★ Contents ★

A Nation Forged by War

The United States, like many nations, was forged and defined by war. Despite Benjamin Franklin's opinion that "There never was a good war or a bad peace," the United States owes its very existence to the War of Independence, one to which Franklin wholeheartedly subscribed. The country forged by war in 1776 was tempered and made stronger by the Civil War in the 1860s.

The Texas Revolution, the Mexican-American War, and the Spanish-American War expanded the country's borders and gave it overseas possessions. These wars made the United States a world power, but this status came with a price, as the nation became a key but reluctant player in both World War I and World War II.

Each successive war further defined the country's role on the world stage. Following World War II, U.S. foreign policy redefined itself to focus on the role of defender, not only of the freedom of its own citizens but also of the freedom of people everywhere. During the Cold War that followed World War II until the collapse of the Soviet Union, defending the world meant fighting communism. This goal, manifested in the Korean and Vietnam conflicts, proved elusive, and soured the American public on its achievability. As the United States emerged as the world's sole superpower, American foreign policy has been guided less by national interest and more on protecting international human rights. But as involvement in Somalia and Kosovo proves, this goal has been equally elusive.

As a result, the country's view of itself changed. Bolstered by victories in World Wars I and II, Americans first relished the role of protector. But, as war followed war in a seemingly endless procession, Americans began to doubt their leaders, their motives, and themselves. The Vietnam War especially caused people to question the validity of sending young people to die in places where they were not particularly wanted and for people who did not seem especially grateful.

While the most obvious changes brought about by America's wars have been geopolitical in nature, many other aspects of society have been touched. War often does not bring about change directly but acts instead like the catalyst in a chemical reaction, accelerating changes already in progress.

Some of these changes have been societal. The role of women in the United States had been slowly changing, but World War II put thousands into the work force and into uniform. They might have gone back to being housewives after the war, but equality, once experienced, would not be forgotten.

Likewise, wars have accelerated technological change. The necessity for faster airplanes and a more destructive bomb led to the development of jet planes and nuclear energy. Artificial fibers developed for parachutes in the 1940s were used in the clothing of the 1950s.

Lucent Books' American War Library covers key wars in the development of the nation. Each war is covered in several volumes to allow for more detail and context and to provide volumes on often neglected subjects, such as the kamikazes of World War II or weapons used in the Civil War. As with all Lucent Books, notes, annotated bibliographies, and appendixes such as glossaries give students a launching point for further research. In addition, sidebars and archival photographs enhance the text. Together, each volume in the American War Library will aid students in understanding how America's wars have shaped and changed its politics, economics, and society.

Weapons Too Terrible to Use

Inherent in warfare throughout the ages has been the quest to find better and more efficient ways for one human to kill another, for one army to annihilate another army, for one nation to subdue another nation. From the first stone thrown in anger by a Neanderthal to the latest stealth bombers, each generation of warrior has hoped to be the one to build the ultimate weapon, the implement of war against which no human, army, or nation can stand. Of all the weapons developed by humans, atomic energy has probably come closer than any other to being the ultimate weapon. The following description bears witness to the awesome power of an atomic explosion:

A moment or so after its explosion began it was still mainly an inert sphere exploding superficially, a big, inanimate nucleus wrapped in flame and thunder. . . . As more of the Carolinum became active the bomb spread itself out into a monstrous cavern of fiery energy at the base of what became very speedily a miniature active volcano. . . . Once launched, the bomb was absolutely unapproachable and uncontrollable until its forces were nearly exhausted, and from the crater that burst open above it, puffs of heavy incandescent vapour and fragments of viciously punitive rock and mud, saturated with Carolinum, and each a centre of scorching and blistering energy, were flung high and far.[1]

This chilling narrative was written not by a scientist or reporter, however, but by a science fiction writer. H.G. Wells, the author of such famous novels as *The War of the Worlds* and *The Time Machine*, included the description in his book *The Last War: The World Set Free*. What is even more remarkable is that the book was

Moments after detonation, an atom bomb explodes and engulfs Bikini Atoll, shooting a mushroom cloud high into the air.

published in 1914, thirty-one years before the first real atomic bomb was exploded. This passage marked the first time that an atomic bomb was described. Wells created the fictitious element Carolinum as the power that made his atomic bomb work. But even as he wrote, scientists such as Marie Curie, Ernest Rutherford, and Niels Bohr were investigating the mysteries of the atom and attempting to unlock its secrets. One wonders if they, like Wells, foresaw the destructive power of the strange new elements that were the objects of their research.

The World Set Free was published on the eve of World War I, the first great global conflict. In Wells's futuristic book, a massive atomic war in 1956 destroys civilization and a new world—a better, more peaceful world—arises from the radioactive ashes. Wells saw the atomic bomb as the ultimate weapon that would create a new society, a world set free from old rivalries and inequalities. Toward the end of World War II, the atomic bomb was seen as a way to bring a swift end to the most devastating war in history. From 1945 to the demise of the Soviet Union in 1991, it was the key piece in the delicate chess game of nuclear politics that was known as the Cold War.

Are atomic weapons truly the ultimate weapons? During the Cold War, the rapid growth of the nuclear arsenals possessed by the world's two superpowers, the United States and the Soviet Union, could have led to an atomic holocaust similar to the one Wells described. In-deed, several times during that forty-six-year period, the two antagonists came close to unleashing these weapons of mass destruction. Scientists designed them, politicians ordered them, and generals deployed them around the world, all the while praying that they would never be used. Fortunately, the sheer magnitude of the destruction brought about by a nuclear war made starting such a war unthinkable. And so, because of their very existence and the devastation they represented, these ultimate weapons of war became, in a real sense, weapons of peace.

Chapter 1

The Ultimate Weapon: The Atomic Bomb

I t was an unlikely location for an event that would change the world. For years, the squash court under the west grandstand of Stagg Field at the University of Chicago remained unused and empty. Athletics had taken a backseat to academics at the prestigious university, but by December 1942, as World War II raged in Europe and the Pacific, the court was once more bustling with activity. It was, however, activity of a different sort, and the participants were not athletes but scientists—the foremost physicists and chemists in the world. Leading the scientific team was a brilliant Italian physicist named Enrico Fermi, who had escaped the oppression of Benito Mussolini's fascist Italy in 1938. Now Fermi and more than forty other people, many of them top scientists in their own fields, stood on a balcony overlooking the squash court. The building was unheated, and on this bitterly cold Chicago morning the group shivered perhaps as much

from apprehension as from the cold. Before them stood a hulking structure made of thousands of black bricks. Measuring twenty-five feet wide and twenty feet tall, it was the world's first atomic reactor. The scientists simply called it the "pile." But within this pile lurked a secret that had enormous implications for the future.

It had been almost a year since the surprise Japanese attack on Pearl Harbor, Hawaii, had drawn the United States into World War II. The United States had joined Great Britain and its ideological opponent, the Communist Soviet Union, against Nazi Germany, Italy, and Japan in the devastating global conflict. WWII was, nevertheless, warfare with conventional weaponry—tanks, warships, artillery, and TNT-based explosives. Now the scientists gathered in the squash court were about to conduct an experiment that, if successful, would lead to a weapon with a destructive power the world had never seen before. The experiment depended on their ability to start and control an atomic chain reaction.

Such a chain reaction, fundamental to the weaponry that distinguishes the Cold War from all other wars, would begin with the tiny building blocks that make up all matter in the universe: the atom.

The Basis of Atomic Weapons

The idea that everything is made up of particles too small to see is as old as ancient Greece. Indeed, it was the Greeks who gave those particles their name: *atomos*, which we now call atoms. The word *atomos* means indivisible; the ancient Greeks believed that nothing was smaller. Modern science, however, has proved

that atoms are not the smallest particles in the universe. They are composed of many tinier subatomic particles, primarily neutrons, protons, and electrons.

In the early 1930s, scientists such as Hungarian-born physicist Leo Szilard began to envision bombarding one atom with a neutron from another. Szilard knew that, in theory, an atom could be split, releasing energy. The first atom would be split in half by the speeding neutron of the second, releasing two neutrons. These two neutrons would split two other atoms,

Leo Szilard studies equations at his desk. He theorized that an atom could be split in half by a neutron of another atom.

which in turn would split even more atoms, and so on. This process, the so-called chain reaction, would release a tremendous amount of energy that could be used either as a source of power for industry or as a fearsome weapon. "I didn't see at the moment . . . what experiments would be needed," Szilard recalled, "but the idea never left me. In certain circumstances it might be possible to set up a nuclear chain reaction, liberate energy on an industrial scale, and construct atomic bombs."[2]

Within a few years, the theory of splitting atoms had become fact, and it had been given a name. In 1938 German scientists Otto Hahn and Fritz Strassmann had been experimenting with the element uranium, a radioactive metal. They bombarded the uranium with neutrons, resulting in the creation of two other elements, barium and krypton. Although they did not realize it, they had actually split the uranium atom. The next year, experiments by Austrian physicists Lise Meitner and Otto Frisch confirmed the idea that a speeding neutron could split a uranium atom, releasing an enormous amount of energy. They called this process "fission," taking the name from the biological process through which living cells divide. Researchers now had scientific evidence that nuclear fission was possible. But would this new discovery be used

for peace or war? German dictator Adolf Hitler would force the answer to that question.

Warning America

As Hitler was assembling his massive military machine in the late 1930s, many people feared that German scientists were already conducting research that could lead to the development of an atomic bomb. Leo Szilard was convinced that U.S. president Franklin D. Roosevelt had to be warned of the impending peril. But

Albert Einstein coauthored a letter with Szilard warning President Franklin Roosevelt of the impending dangers of atomic energy.

Szilard was virtually unknown outside of scientific circles and had little hope of actually meeting Roosevelt. So he turned for help to the most famous and respected physicist in the world, Albert Einstein. On August 2, 1939, Szilard and Einstein drafted a letter warning Roosevelt of the potential dangers of atomic energy. The letter was signed by Einstein and intended to be hand-carried to President Roosevelt by Alexander Sachs, one of the president's trusted advisers. But world events delayed the delivery of the letter. On September 1, 1939, Hitler's army invaded Poland, marking the beginning of World War II. When Sachs finally delivered the letter to Roosevelt on October 11, 1939, the president remarked, "Alex, what you are after is to see that the Nazis don't blow us up." Roosevelt turned to his secretary Edwin "Pa" Watson and said, "Pa, this requires action."[3] With these words, Roosevelt began his own chain reaction that would create a top-secret project to produce an atomic bomb.

The Manhattan Project

In October 1939 an Advisory Committee on Uranium was formed to study the problems involved in splitting uranium atoms. In June 1942, upon the recommendation of the Advisory Committee, Roosevelt established America's official atomic bomb project and placed it under the supervision of the Army Corps of Engineers. The code name for the project was the Manhattan Engineer District, a

purposely nondescript title taken from the New York borough where its original headquarters were located. But it was most often referred to simply as the Manhattan Project. Such an important project needed a strong leader to guide it, and for the Manhattan Project that leader was a gruff, heavy-set army colonel named Leslie R. Groves.

As deputy chief of construction for the Army Corps of Engineers, Groves had just completed supervising the building of the new military headquarters, the Pentagon, and was eager for a chance to get into the war in Europe. But his commanding officer, General Brehon Somervell, had other plans: "The Secretary of War has selected you for a very important assignment, and the President has approved the selection."[4] The important assignment was to head up the Manhattan Project. Groves's immediate reaction was a somewhat less than enthusiastic, "Oh, that thing."[5] He later described himself as "probably the angriest officer in the United States Army."[6] Groves's new duty would keep him in the United States, where he would oversee the construction of factories to produce the fissionable material needed for the atomic bomb and guide the bomb project to completion. In recognition of the importance of his new responsibilities, Groves was promoted to brigadier general.

Despite his initial reluctance, Groves was the right man for the job. Lieutenant Colonel Keith Nichols, who worked under

Groves on the project, described him as "one of the most capable individuals [I've ever met]. He had an ego second to none, he had tireless energy. . . . He had absolute confidence in his decisions and he was absolutely ruthless in how he approached a problem to get it done."[7] These personality traits would ruffle many feathers along the way, but they were just what was needed to get the bomb built. Groves officially took over the Manhattan Project on September 23, 1942, and three months later the atomic reactor was given its first test.

Fermi's Pile

The crude version of what would be called a nuclear reactor today, the "pile" that stood on the squash court under the stands at the University of Chicago was just that, a pile of black bricks arranged layer after layer until it was an egg-shaped construction some fifty-seven layers high. Alternating with layers of plain bricks were layers drilled to hold spheres of uranium—the radioactive material that emits the neutrons with which Fermi hoped to create a self-sustaining chain reaction.

The bricks in the pile were made of graphite, the soft form of carbon commonly used for pencil lead. These graphite bricks were greasy and difficult to handle for the workers who built the pile but necessary to increase the chance of nuclear fission. The floor of the squash court became slippery, and the walls turned black. Leona Woods, a graduate student and one of the few women working on the pile, described the scene: "Everything and everybody soon became black with graphite dust. There was a black haze in the air that scattered the beams from the floodlights. . . . The only white to be seen was now and then the gleam of someone's teeth."[8]

The Italian Navigator Arrives

On the morning of December 2, 1942, everything was ready. After Fermi's team had gathered on the balcony of the squash court, the control rods, long wooden sticks covered in cadmium, called control rods because they could be pushed and pulled in and out of the pile to control the rate of reaction, were withdrawn from the pile.

The clicking of the neutron counters increased in speed as the neutron bombardment in the pile grew. Soon the scientists had to switch to a different instrument, a chart recorder, to keep up with the pile. But the recorder's pen could not keep up as the radiation levels rose. Fermi's Chicago colleague Herbert Anderson described the scene as the critical moment approached: "Again and again, the recorder's scale had to be changed to accommodate the neutron intensity which was increasing more and more rapidly. Suddenly Fermi raised his hand. 'The pile has gone critical,' he announced. No one present had any doubt about it."[9] The world's first self-sustaining chain reaction had just taken place.

Arthur H. Compton, the overall head of the project at the University of Chicago, telephoned Washington to report Fermi's success. In keeping with the secrecy of the project, his announcement was couched in code: "The Italian navigator has just landed in the new world. . . . Everyone landed safe and happy."[10] And yet, not everyone involved with the pile

Enrico Fermi's Pile scientists, builders of the first atomic reactor, gather outside the University of Chicago.

was encouraged by the results. Leo Szilard, who had envisioned the use of atomic energy for peaceful purposes, knew that the road from Chicago would lead instead to an atomic bomb. When the others had left the squash court, Szilard stayed behind. "I shook hands with Fermi," he recalled, "and I said I thought this day would go down as a black day in the history of mankind."[11]

The successful chain reaction indicated that, in theory, an atomic bomb would work. Now it was up to General Leslie Groves to turn that theory into reality.

Uranium and Plutonium

The essential ingredient of a nuclear reactor or an atomic bomb is a radioactive material that causes the chain reaction by emitting neutrons. In the Chicago pile, that material was uranium, specifically a special type of uranium called U-235. But U-235 had to be refined from natural uranium ore, a difficult process that yielded only minute quantities of the fissionable substance. Scientists searched to find other elements that might also be suitable material for a bomb. In 1940 chemist Glenn T. Seaborg discovered that plutonium, another radioactive element, was created when uranium atoms were subjected to neutron bombardment. Thus, plutonium, which is extremely rare in nature, could be created in a nuclear reactor similar to Fermi's pile. Plutonium, or Pu-239, fissioned even more readily than U-235, making it an ideal material for an atomic bomb. One of General Groves's first priorities as head of the Manhattan Project was to set up facilities to create U-235 and Pu-239.

Even before Groves had pinned on his general's stars, he gave his approval for the purchase of more than fifty thousand acres of land near Knoxville in eastern Tennessee. On this site, officially called the Clinton Engineer Works but commonly known as Oak Ridge (for the Black Oak Ridge that ran nearby), research laboratories, factories, warehouses, and living quarters for thousands of workers would spring up. In August 1943 Oak Ridge began its primary task: to produce U-235 for the atomic bomb. It had been planned for Oak Ridge to pioneer the production of plutonium, but Groves soon realized that the job was too big and too dangerous for the Tennessee site. "If . . . a reactor were to explode," Groves said, "and throw great quantities of highly radioactive materials into the atmosphere when the wind was blowing toward Knoxville, the loss of life and the damage to health in the area might be catastrophic."[12] Therefore, another facility would be needed, and Groves found the perfect location in the Columbia River Basin of Washington State. The area near a small town named Hanford in southeastern Washington met all of Groves's criteria for isolation and the availability of sufficient water and electric power. In the summer of 1943, construction began on the laboratories, residences, and the reactors that would produce plutonium for the atomic bomb.

While Oak Ridge and Hanford made the raw materials of uranium and pluto-

Using tongs, a scientist of the Oak Ridge laboratories introduces plutonium through the top of a reactor.

nium, General Groves pondered the question of where the bomb should be built. As it turned out, a tall, lanky, and brilliant physicist named Oppenheimer would provide the answer.

Los Alamos

J. Robert Oppenheimer was a professor of theoretical physics at the University of California at Berkeley. Like the University of Chicago, Berkeley was one of many institutions around the country working on various aspects of bomb development for the Manhattan Project. General Groves needed a top physicist to direct the actual construction of the bomb, and he chose Oppenheimer for the job, despite some reservations. He knew that Oppenheimer "was well qualified to handle the theoretical aspects of the work, but how he would do on the practical experimentation, or how he would handle the administrative responsibilities, [Groves] had no

The Father of the Atomic Bomb

When J. Robert Oppenheimer, top Manhattan Project scientist, observed the test explosion of the first atomic bomb at Trinity, he commented, "I am become Death, the destroyer of worlds." The words, quoted in Richard Rhodes's book, *The Making of the Atomic Bomb,* were from the Bhagavad-Gita, a sacred Hindu text, and they typified the broad education and introspective nature of the man who led the scientific effort to build the atomic bomb.

Robert Oppenheimer (he rarely used his first initial) was born in New York City on April 22, 1904. His father was a wealthy Jewish textile importer, his mother a talented artist. As a child Robert became fascinated with science, developing such a keen interest in mineralogy that he presented a scientific paper to the New York Mineralogical Club at age twelve. He attended the Ethical Culture School in New York from second grade through high school where he studied classical literature and languages as well as science and mathematics. Although Robert's intelligence impressed adults, he had difficulty making friends his own age. A frail youth, Robert went to a New Mexico ranch one summer to rejuvenate his health. Thus began his lifelong love of the New Mexican desert country, which played a part in the decision to locate the Manhattan Project laboratory at Los Alamos.

After earning his Ph.D. from the University of Göttingen in Germany, Oppenheimer taught physics until 1942, when he was chosen by General Leslie Groves to head the scientific work of the Manhattan Project. "Oppie," as his colleagues at Los Alamos called him, got the job done, but a shadow of suspicion formed over his later career. His opposition to the hydrogen bomb and previous associations with Communists led in the early 1950s to a charge of disloyalty. A hearing in 1954 cleared Oppenheimer of the disloyalty charge, but the U.S. government revoked his security clearance. After returning to academic life, Oppenheimer died in 1967.

Although he was a brilliant physicist, J. Robert Oppenheimer never won the coveted Nobel Prize. But as the "father of the atomic bomb," his contribution to history will not be forgotten.

J. Robert Oppenheimer developed the atomic bomb.

idea."[13] Still, there were no better candidates, so in October 1942 Oppenheimer became head of the scientific division of the Manhattan Project.

Groves realized that he would need to set up a laboratory for the actual construction of the bomb. It would have to be isolated for safety and security reasons and have an adequate water supply, nearby railroad lines, and year-round good weather. After several sites in the southwestern United States had been considered and rejected, Oppenheimer came up with the ideal location: a former boys' boarding school on an isolated plateau in northern New Mexico called Los Alamos.

Once the location had been determined, Groves and Oppenheimer began assembling a team to construct the bomb. Physicists, chemists, engineers, machinists, clerks, laborers, and military personnel all played vital roles in the Manhattan Project. Security was tight: Scientists used false identities and the weapon they were developing was always called "the gadget," never a bomb. Nevertheless, within the Los Alamos team

were people intent on delivering information to the Soviet Union, still officially an American ally but a party to none of the secret research.

Spies at Los Alamos

Among the scientists at Los Alamos was a young physicist named Klaus Fuchs. A quiet, balding man who wore wire-rimmed glasses, Fuchs was born in Germany in 1911. As a young man he joined the German Communist Party but was forced to flee that country in 1933 when Hitler came to power and began persecuting Communists. Settling in Britain,

Klaus Fuchs, a scientist at Los Alamos, worked as a Soviet spy during World War II.

Fuchs continued his university studies, ultimately becoming a noted physicist. With the German invasion of the Soviet Union in World War II, he decided he could help the Soviet war effort by spying.

Fuchs came to the United States in 1943 as part of a group of British physicists collaborating with U.S. scientists on the atomic bomb. The British scientific group first worked in New York, where Fuchs began giving secret reports and other documents to a contact he knew only as "Raymond." Raymond was actually a Soviet agent named Harry Gold, who passed along the classified information to the Soviet Union and the scientists there who were working on their own atomic bomb program. In August 1944, when the British group moved to Los Alamos, Fuchs continued to pass secret information to Harry Gold, including a sketch of the device and its parts, with dimensions.

Oppie's Soviet Counterpart

Although thousands of people took part in the Manhattan Project, physicist J. Robert Oppenheimer was ultimately accountable for the success or failure of America's atomic bomb program. When the Soviet Union began its quest for the atom bomb, the ultimate responsibility for the task also was given to a physicist, but with one significant difference—the Russian would either succeed at the job or likely die trying.

Igor Vasilievich Kurchatov was born on January 12, 1903, in a small town in the southern Ural Mountains of the Soviet Union. The second of three children, Igor was an excellent student and planned on a career in engineering. He graduated from Crimea State University in three years and then studied nautical engineering in Petrograd. Soon, however, Kurchatov's interests turned to the emerging field of atomic physics. At the Soviet Institute of Physics and Technology he performed experiments in radiation, ultimately becoming head of the nuclear physics department. He was named director of the Soviet Union's atomic bomb program in 1942, the same year that Oppenheimer became head of the Manhattan Project.

Although Kurchatov, like Oppenheimer, was a skilled physicist, his outgoing personality was vastly different from the introspective nature of his American counterpart. Lively, cheerful, and possessing a quick wit, the bearded Kurchatov never put on airs. His expertise in physics and organizational ability made him an ideal choice to head the Soviet atomic bomb project. But Kurchatov had another, more personal, reason to succeed: Soviet scientists who failed to produce results were usually shot by dictator Joseph Stalin's ruthless henchmen.

Kurchatov did succeed, with the help of secrets stolen from the Manhattan Project by Soviet spies. When the Soviet Union exploded its first atomic bomb in 1949, Kurchatov, perhaps understandably, rejoiced. While Oppenheimer later spoke out against the development of a U.S. hydrogen bomb, Kurchatov helped the Soviet Union build its own thermonuclear weapon.

Kurchatov spent his later years working on the peaceful uses of nuclear energy. When he died in 1960, he was given a hero's burial in the wall of the Kremlin. Before his death, Igor Kurchatov said that he believed his research would be used only for the benefit of mankind. But it was, in fact, the first step in an arms race that would soon threaten mankind's very existence.

Klaus Fuchs was not the only Soviet spy in the Manhattan Project. David Greenglass, a machinist at Los Alamos, gave away classified information as well, including a drawing of a critical part of the bomb and a plan of the Los Alamos facility. Greenglass's sister, New Yorker Ethel Rosenberg, and her husband, Julius, were accused of passing atomic secrets to the Soviet Union. Ted Hall, a junior scientist with Soviet sympathies at Los Alamos, also passed on secret Manhattan Project documents.

It is difficult to understand how so many Soviet agents were able to penetrate the tight security of the Manhattan Project. It is just as difficult to know exactly how helpful their espionage was to the Soviets. Igor Kurchatov, head of the Soviet Union's atomic bomb program, later stated that Klaus Fuchs's reports were of significant, exceptional importance. At the time, it was estimated that espionage activities saved Soviet scientists one to two years' work in their atomic bomb program.

Little Boy and Fat Man

As World War II raged throughout 1943 and 1944, scientists at Oak Ridge, Hanford, and Los Alamos worked tirelessly on the atomic bomb project. Things did not always go smoothly. The Oak Ridge facility was having trouble producing more than minute amounts of the bomb-grade uranium needed, and it was estimated that by mid-1945 there would be enough fissionable material for only one bomb. At Hanford, reactor problems hampered progress, but large-scale plutonium production finally began in December 1944. For these two kinds of nuclear material, two different types of bombs were developed.

The uranium would be used in what was called a "gun-type" bomb. Inside the bomb, a detonator would fire a uranium projectile through a gun barrel into a uranium target. The combined pieces would reach a critical mass, creating a chain reaction and its resulting atomic explosion. Because it was the smaller of the two bombs, it was nicknamed "Little Boy." The scientists at Los Alamos determined that a gun-type bomb would not work with plutonium. So they designed an "implosion-type" bomb. In this configuration, a core of plutonium was surrounded by specially shaped charges of high explosives called "lenses." When these explosives were detonated, the pressure of the inward-focused blast, or implosion, would compress the plutonium. Upon reaching its critical mass, the bomb would explode. This bomb, fatter and rounder than the uranium bomb, was called "Fat Man."

After years of work, Manhattan Project physicists were fairly confident that the gun-type gadget would work. But they were not as sure about the implosion gadget, and they decided that a test was needed to find out. For this test they chose a desert site in southern New

Mexico. J. Robert Oppenheimer named the test "Trinity."

Little Boy, the first uranium "gun-type" atomic bomb, hangs in the laboratory at Los Alamos.

Trinity

The area chosen for the world's first atomic bomb test was a barren desert valley near Alamogordo, some two hundred miles south of Los Alamos, called Jornada del Muerto. By November 1944, workers were busy building concrete command and observation bunkers and assembling a one-hundred-foot steel tower topped with a covered oak platform. On the platform, the Fat Man plutonium bomb would be hoisted and, if all went accord-

ing to plan, detonated. This was "ground zero" at the Trinity site.

Thunder and lightning crackled through the predawn skies on July 16, 1945, the day of the Trinity test. That morning, many of the scientists, military men, and other observers wondered if the test might be postponed. "It was raining cats and dogs," recalled physicist Isidor Rabi as he nervously waited. "[We were] really scared [that] this object there in the tower might be set off accidentally."[14] But the storm finally moved on, and the countdown began. In the command bunker ten thousand yards from ground zero, Oppenheimer watched as the automatic timers relentlessly marched toward zero. General Thomas Farrell noted that Oppenheimer "grew tenser as the last seconds ticked off. He scarcely breathed. He held on to a post to steady himself. For the last few seconds he stared directly ahead."[15]

At 5:29:45 Mountain War Time, a light brighter than a thousand suns turned night into day. As Rabi described it, "Suddenly, there was an enormous flash of light, the brightest light I have ever seen or that I think anyone has ever seen. It blasted; it pounced; it bored its way right through you."[16] A huge mushroom-shaped cloud boiled up over the Jornada del Muerto, rising more than forty thousand feet into the sky in shades of gold, blue, and purple. The shock wave came about forty seconds later, a blast

Fat Man contained plutonium surrounded by high-explosive lenses to create a larger "implosion-type" atomic bomb.

that knocked at least one observer off his feet. The tower on which Fat Man had rested was vaporized, and the sand at ground zero fused into a green glasslike substance later named Trinitite. General Farrell turned to Groves and said, "The war is over." Groves replied, "Yes, after we drop two bombs on Japan."[17]

Hiroshima and Nagasaki

Three weeks later, high above the Japanese city of Hiroshima, three silver airplanes, American B-29 Superfortresses, were tiny specks crossing a cloudless summer sky. Few on the city streets below paid much attention to the "B-sans," as the Japanese called them. No sirens wailed, for air raids usually involved not just three but dozens or even hundreds of planes. Yet the bomb bay of the *Enola Gay*, one of the B-29s, contained the weapon that would destroy the city of Hiroshima: Little Boy, the gun-type uranium bomb developed by the Manhattan Project.

August 6, 1945, 8:16:02 A.M. In a momentary flash of incredible light, Little

The Doomsday Clock

The Educational Foundation for Nuclear Science is a nonprofit organization devoted to education about the danger of nuclear weapons. Founded in 1945, the foundation publishes the influential monthly *Bulletin of the Atomic Scientists*. In 1947 the *Bulletin* first displayed a striking piece of cover art that became an enduring symbol of the atomic age throughout the Cold War and to the present day.

The drawing on the cover was the upper left quarter of a clock face, showing the hours between nine and twelve o'clock. The hands of the clock register the degree of nuclear danger the world faces by how close they are pointing to midnight, the implied "hour of doom." Not surprisingly, the clock is often referred to as the "Doomsday Clock." Artist Martyl Langsdorf, the designer of the clock, was the wife of a Manhattan Project scientist. For the first appearance of the clock in 1947, she drew the hands at seven minutes to midnight. As the *Bulletin*'s website (www.thebulletin.org) explains, "While Martyl intended the clock image as a whole to convey a sense of imminent danger, placing the minute hand at seven minutes to midnight was a matter of 'good design.' The idea of moving the minute hand came later, in 1949, as a way to dramatize the magazine's response to world peril."

During the Cold War years, the *Bulletin* clock's minute hand was moved fourteen times as the conflict between the superpowers alternately heated up and cooled down. Just two years after the Doomsday Clock first appeared, the hand was moved to three minutes to midnight, a reaction to the test of the first Soviet atomic bomb. The closest the clock's hands came to midnight was two minutes in 1953, the year when the United States and the Soviet Union both detonated hydrogen bombs. It has been as far away as seventeen minutes in 1991. Surprisingly, during the Cuban Missile Crisis of 1963, when the world was its closest to nuclear war, the hands were back to seven minutes before midnight. When arms control treaties were signed, the hands would retreat; as nuclear arsenals grew and world conflicts increased, the hands advanced once more toward a nuclear midnight.

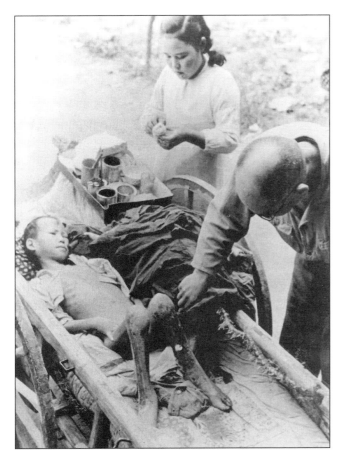

Physicians attend to a young boy after the American nuclear attack on Japan.

Boy exploded some two thousand feet above Hiroshima. The blast was the equivalent of fifteen thousand tons of TNT.

Approximately 70,000 people perished that morning or within a few days; in all, some 140,000 would die by the end of the year. In a moment, Hiroshima was reduced to charred and burning rubble. It would take another atomic bomb, the plutonium Fat Man dropped on Nagasaki three days later, to convince Japanese emperor Hirohito to surrender, ending World War II but not the adversarial politics that characterized the atomic age.

After the war, Oppenheimer said, "When it went off, in the New Mexico dawn, that first atomic bomb, we thought of Alfred Nobel, and his hope, his vain hope, that dynamite would put an end to wars. We thought . . . of that deep sense of guilt in man's new powers, that reflects his recognition of evil, and his long knowledge of it. We knew that it was a new world."[18]

For the next forty years, Oppenheimer's new world would be dominated by nuclear weapons and the race to develop them.

Chapter 2

Airborne Weaponry

he end of World War II marked the immediate beginning of another war, one that would last longer than any other war in American history. It was called the Cold War because it was mainly a war of politics and ideologies rather than military battles. But weapons did play an important part in the Cold War, especially the atomic weapons created by the scientists of the Manhattan Project. At the close of World War II, the United States was the world's only "superpower," the sole nation to possess atomic weapons. But America's nuclear monopoly would soon end, as the Soviet Union was diligently working, also in secret, to become the world's second superpower, and both powers developed the means to drop atomic bombs from sophisticated aircraft.

Truman and the Bomb

In the spring of 1945, as the European phase of World War II was drawing to a close, wartime president Franklin D. Roosevelt, who had initiated the Manhattan Project, died; less than three hours later, Harry S. Truman, Roosevelt's vice president, took the oath of office. Truman, a plain-spoken bespectacled man from Missouri, was now the thirty-third president of the United States.

Since the president is also the commander-in-chief in charge of the nation's armed forces, Truman had to be brought up to date on U.S. military activities. That meant he had to be told about the atomic bomb. Even as vice president, Truman knew little more about the top-secret Manhattan Project than that it existed. So on April 25, 1945, Secretary of War Henry L. Stimson and General Leslie Groves met the new president at the White House. "Within four months," Stimson began, reading from a memorandum he had written, "we shall in all probability have completed the most terrible weapon ever known in human history, one bomb of which could destroy a whole city."[19] Truman listened as Stimson and Groves explained the details of the atomic bomb project, asking occasional questions to clarify points he did not understand. Stimson warned that the United States would not always be the only nation with atomic weapons and that "probably the only nation which could enter production within the next few years is Russia."[20] Little did he realize that Soviet undercover agents had already infiltrated the Manhattan Project and were stealing vital atomic secrets. But while the Soviets were secretly developing their bomb, the United States was working on its own problem: how to set up an efficient delivery system for the bomb it already had.

"Peace Is Our Profession"

After World War II, the U.S. military began to reorganize for its new mission of defending America in the postwar world. On March 21, 1946, the Strategic Air Command (SAC) was formed as a part of the Army Air Force (which would

President Harry S. Truman, shortly after succeeding Franklin Roosevelt, made the decision to drop the atomic bomb.

The Baruch Plan

On October 24, 1945, a new international organization known as the United Nations was officially founded. Dedicated to promoting cooperation between nations and solving international problems, the UN began with fifty-one member nations, including the United States and the Soviet Union. In recognition of the danger posed by the atomic bomb, one of the first acts of the new organization was to create the United Nations Atomic Energy Commission. The commission's twofold mission was to seek a ban on atomic weapons and promote the peaceful use of atomic energy. On June 14, 1946, the U.S. representative, Bernard Baruch, addressed the commission with a plan for regulating atomic power. His complete remarks, from which the following is taken, can be found at the Nuclear Age Peace Foundation website (www.nuclearfiles.org):

> We are here to make a choice between the quick and the dead. That is our business. . . . We find ourselves here to test if man can produce, through his will and faith, the miracle of peace, just as he has, through science and skill, the miracle of the atom. . . . We of this nation, desirous of helping to bring peace to the world and realizing the heavy obligations upon us arising from our possession of the means of producing the bomb and from the fact that it is part of our armament, are prepared to make our full contribution toward effective control of atomic energy.

The Baruch Plan, as it was known, would establish an organization called the International Atomic Development Authority (IADA) to oversee the world's atomic energy. Atomic weapons would be banned, and the acquiring of nuclear materials such as uranium and plutonium would rest with the IADA, not with individual nations. All research for the peaceful use of atomic energy would be carried out by the organization. In addition, the IADA would have the right to perform inspections of any country to make sure no atomic weapons were being built and to punish those nations that violated the agreement.

It was remarkable that the United States, as the sole atomic power in 1946, would give up that monopoly for the cause of world peace. Not only would all U.S. atomic bombs be dismantled, but the United States would give the IADA the results of the nuclear research it had developed through the Manhattan Project. Of the atomic bomb, Bernard Baruch said that the United States "stands ready to proscribe [ban] this instrument—to lift its use from death to life—if the world will join in a pact to that end." While many nations were indeed willing to join that pact, the Soviet Union balked. Soviet leaders were concerned that the inspectors called for in the plan might actually be agents sent to spy on Soviet industrial and military installations. Instead, they proposed an alternate plan that eliminated inspections and punishment for disobedient nations. The United States rejected the Soviet plan, and the world's first effort to eliminate nuclear arms reached a stalemate.

become the United States Air Force in 1947). The Strategic Air Command slogan, "Peace Is Our Profession," was a concise statement of the organization's primary purpose. SAC's official mission, as defined by General Carl Spaatz, the

commander of the Army Air Force, was "to conduct long-range offensive operations in any part of the world . . . to conduct maximum range reconnaissance over land or sea . . . to provide combat units capable of intense and sustained combat operations employing the latest and most advanced weapons."[21]

Defining the Triad

One of SAC's bombers, the B-29 Superfortress, was the aircraft that dropped the atomic bombs on Japan. The long-distance bombers of the Strategic Air Command were the first leg of the U.S. military force structure called the "triad." Developed in the early 1960s and still operational today, the triad is based on three separate strategic components: airborne nuclear bombers, ground-based missiles, and sea-based missiles. Each leg of the triad compensates for a weakness

in the others. For example, ground-based missiles are highly accurate and ready for virtually immediate launch in an alert. But they are impossible to recall once launched, and their fixed locations make them vulnerable to enemy attack. Sea-based missiles carried on submarines are less accurate, but because they are extremely difficult for the enemy to detect, they are almost invulnerable. Bombers take longer to reach their targets, but they are the most flexible leg of the triad,

Part of the Strategic Air Command's first leg of the Triad, the B-29 Superfortress, dropped an enormous number of bombs.

able to change targets or even abort a mission at the last minute if the situation warrants.

However, since the B-29 was originally designed to carry many smaller, conventional bombs instead of the large and heavy Little Boy or Fat Man, the aircraft had to be converted for atomic use. Engine and propeller modifications were made, and the bomb bay was redesigned to accommodate atomic bombs. Space for the extra crewman needed to monitor the bombs was created in the plane's forward section. The B-29 eventually evolved into an aircraft designated B-50, an upgraded version of the Superfortress specifically designed to carry atomic payloads.

In June 1948 a new bomber, the B-36 Peacemaker, joined the Strategic Air Command fleet. With a wingspan of 230 feet, the B-36 was the largest piston-engined bomber ever built, dwarfing the B-29. It was also the first truly intercontinental bomber, with a range of approximately seventy-five hundred miles—enough to deliver atomic bombs to the Soviet Union. Propelled by six piston engines, with a pair of turbojet engines under each wing to assist at takeoff and at other crucial moments, the B-36 could carry massive bomb loads of up to eighty-six thousand pounds.

Delivering the Bomb

The B-29 Superfortress was the Strategic Air Command's primary weapon in the early days of the Cold War. General Curtis LeMay, the commander of SAC from 1948 to 1957, recalled in his book *Superfortress: The Story of the B-29 and American Air Power* that the B-29 was "the best strategic bomber in the world." It was also the most advanced aircraft of its day.

The B-29 was powered by four piston engines mounted on wings that spanned 141 feet. The Superfortress had pressurized crew spaces, so it could fly in the cold, thin air at high altitudes without the necessity of heavy clothing and oxygen masks for the crew. Therefore, the B-29 was able to operate above bad weather and perform high-altitude bombing runs farther out of reach of antiaircraft artillery. During the Korean War, from 1950 to 1953, Superfortresses flew thousands of hours of combat missions, dropping more than 28 million pounds of conventional bombs. For SAC, however, the main advantage of the B-29 Superfortress was that it was large enough to carry an atomic bomb.

Developing a Nuclear Strategy: Deterrence

The B-36 Peacemaker served SAC from 1948 to 1959. During that time, it was the first line of deterrence against possible Soviet aggression. Deterrence meant that, since the Soviet Union knew the United States had the means to retaliate if it were attacked, the Soviets would be deterred, or prevented from, initiating hostilities. Just the threat of nuclear retaliation, so the theory went, would prevent an all-out war. Deterrence became an official U.S. policy in November 1948.

By the beginning of 1949, the United States had 110 atomic bombs and more than 120 planes to deliver them. The

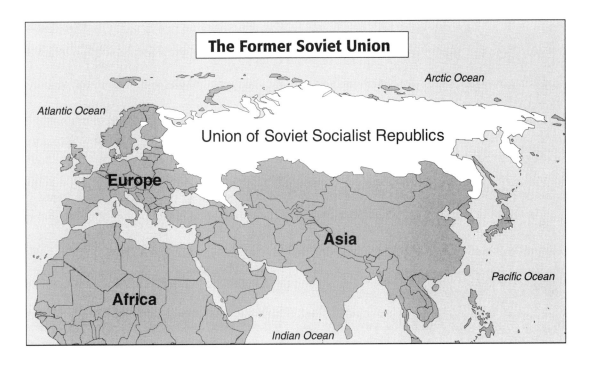

The Former Soviet Union

Arctic Ocean

Atlantic Ocean

Union of Soviet Socialist Republics

Europe

Asia

Pacific Ocean

Africa

Indian Ocean

Soviet Union still did not have a single atomic bomb. But their scientists were coming close to testing one, and the nuclear monopoly enjoyed by the United States at the end of the war would not last long.

"First Lightning"

Like the Manhattan Project, the Soviet atomic bomb program needed a facility for research and testing. The United States had built its atomic laboratory at Los Alamos; the Soviets built theirs at Arzamas. Located some 250 miles east of Moscow, the facility, named for a nearby city, was officially designated Arzamas-16. Soviet physicists had been working on the theoretical aspects of atomic weapons

since 1943, with the help of the spies at Los Alamos. But when Arzamas-16 began operation on April 13, 1946, the program went into high gear. As one engineer wrote, "The security of the country and patriotic duty demanded that we create the atomic bomb. . . . Who would forgive the leadership of the country if it began to create the weapons only after the enemy had decided to attack?"[22]

Even with information supplied by Klaus Fuchs and other spies, it took project head Igor Kurchatov and his scientists years of research and testing to perfect the first Soviet atomic bomb. Modeled after the American Fat Man bomb, the Soviet bomb had a plutonium core. As in the U.S. Trinity test, the bomb would be detonated by implosion at the top of a test tower. A site was prepared near the town of Semipalatinsk on the plains of Kazakhstan, and the test, code-named "First Lightning," was scheduled.

At 7:00 on the morning of August 29, 1949, a brilliant flash illuminated the morning sky over the Semipalatinsk test site. A mushroom cloud of radioactive debris, the now-familiar symbol of an atomic explosion, rose over the place where the test tower once stood. In a scene reminiscent of the relief and exhilaration the American scientists felt after Trinity, Kurchatov and his team rejoiced at the success of their atomic bomb test. "When we succeeded in solving this problem," recalled one physicist, "we felt relief, even happiness—for in possessing such a weapon we had removed the possibility of its being used against the USSR [Soviet Union] with impunity."[23] There were now two superpowers in the world. The threat that each one could annihilate the other, and perhaps destroy the world, in a nuclear holocaust set up the axis of Cold War conflict that would last more than forty years.

On September 23, 1949, less than a month after the Soviets' First Lightning test, President Truman released a statement to the press reporting that "We have evidence that within recent weeks an atomic explosion occurred in the U.S.S.R."[24] Although not unexpected by scientists and military officials in the United States, the Soviet test came sooner than anyone had predicted. The threat was made more real by the knowledge that the Soviets already were producing the bombers to carry and deliver their weapons.

Bulls and Bears

In the summer of 1947 a new Russian bomber called the Tupolev Tu-4 had taken off on its maiden test flight over the Soviet Union. Had any American aviator witnessed this flight, he would have thought he was seeing a B-29 Superfortress. The similarity was no coincidence; the design of the Tu-4 was copied directly from American B-29s that had made emergency landings in the Soviet Union. The Soviets had released the crews but kept the aircraft, using them as a model for their own long-range bomber. In August 1947 the Tu-4 made its first public appearance in a flight over Moscow, and in 1948 it entered into service with the Soviet Air Force.

Nicknamed the Bull, the Tu-4 was not an exact duplicate of the B-29. During its manufacture, workers had to convert U.S. measurements into the metric system used in the Soviet Union. The plane was also modified to accommodate Soviet armament, and it used Soviet engines. But its range and bomb-carrying capacity were similar enough to the B-29 to worry the Strategic Air Command. The Soviet Union now had its first bomber that could reach the United States, even though it would have to be a one-way suicide mission.

Other Soviet aircraft followed the Bull. The Tu-95 Bear was a propeller-driven aircraft with a range of more than eight thousand miles, making it a true intercontinental bomber. Operated by a crew of eight, the Bear could carry twenty-six thousand pounds of nuclear bombs to its target. It was introduced into the Soviet arsenal in 1957 and with various modifications served as a bomber, a reconnaissance aircraft, and a submarine hunter-killer. The Bear was probably the most successful bomber in the Soviet Air Force.

While the Soviets were building new planes, SAC was not standing still in the area of aircraft development. And its newest planes would leave the world of piston-powered aviation behind.

Into the Jet Age

In October 1951 the Strategic Air Command's first jet bomber, the B-47 Stratojet, went into service. As described by aviation historian Bill Gunston, the

The first jet bomber, the B-47 Stratojet, rolls off the assembly line.

Stratojet was "a design so advanced technically as to appear genuinely futuristic."[25] Powered by six jet engines, this sleek aircraft had swept-back wings, which provided improved aerodynamic performance. The Stratojet's maximum speed was about six hundred miles per hour, more than two hundred miles per hour faster than the B-29. It was operated by a crew of three (compared to ten in the B-29) and could carry a payload of up to twenty thousand pounds of conventional bombs, or two atomic bombs.

As an intermediate-range bomber with an operating limit of four thousand miles, the B-47 could not reach targets in the Soviet Union from the United States. Thus, the Stratojet operated from overseas bases in Europe and North Africa. For true intercontinental operations, the B-52 Stratofortress became the Strategic Air Command's primary jet aircraft. The Stratofortress entered SAC's arsenal in June 1955. A strategic bomber with a 185-foot wingspan, the B-52 was powered by eight jet engines that could speed the aircraft to more than six hundred miles per hour. Manned by a crew of five, the B-52 could make a ten-thousand-mile round trip to drop a fifty thousand-pound bomb load on enemy targets and return home safely. The B-52 shared its strategic deterrent role with the B-36 Peacemaker until 1959, when the latter aircraft was retired and SAC became an all-jet force.

The Soviet Union also had been working on jet aircraft, beginning in the early 1950s. The Mya-4 Bison was the first Soviet jet bomber, joining the Soviet air arsenal in 1956. The swept-wing Bison was powered by four jet engines and could carry a twenty-five-ton nuclear payload more than seven thousand miles, or even farther with aerial refueling. The Bison was similar in size to the U.S. B-52 but carried a smaller bomb load. Nevertheless, it was a formidable weapon for the Soviet Union and a challenge for SAC.

Building the "Super"

The Soviet atomic capability forced President Truman to make a decision about an even more deadly weapon: the hydrogen bomb, whose existence had been posed in the early years of World War II. In late 1941 Enrico Fermi had suggested that an atomic bomb might be used to trigger an even larger, more deadly bomb. The Little Boy and Fat Man bombs dropped on Japan worked by fission, or the splitting apart of a heavy atom's nucleus. Instead of fission, the new bomb would create its explosion by fusion. Fusion is the fusing, or joining together, of the atomic nuclei of a light element such as hydrogen. The blast resulting from a fusion reaction can be up to a thousand times greater than that of an atomic bomb. Since fusion is the energy that provides the heat and light in the sun, the hydrogen bomb, or H-bomb, was also called a thermonuclear bomb. But it was also often referred to as the "superbomb," or simply the "super."

Within the Manhattan Project, a small group of physicists had begun theoretical work on the design of a superbomb shortly after the United States entered WW II. Oppenheimer placed Hungarian-born physicist Edward Teller in charge of the "super group." Teller's early calculations showed that an atomic detonation could be used to create the intense heat required to ignite a fusion bomb. He pre-

Scientist Edward Teller took charge of the "super group" of the Manhattan Project.

sented his ideas to a conference of Manhattan Project scientists in the summer of 1942. "My theories were strongly criticized by others in the group," Teller later recalled, "but with the new difficulties, new solutions arose. . . . We were all convinced, by summer's end, that we could accomplish a thermonuclear explosion—and that it would not be too difficult."[26] But it turned out to be more difficult than he realized, and it was soon clear that the hydrogen bomb could not be completed before the war's end.

Code Name Mike

In January 1950 Truman announced, "I have directed the [U.S.] Atomic Energy Commission to continue its work on all forms of atomic weapons, including the so-called hydrogen or superbomb."[27] By late 1952 the first thermonuclear device, based on a design by Teller and mathematician Stanislaw Ulam, was ready to be tested. The bomb used liquid deuterium, a form of hydrogen, as its nuclear fuel. The deuterium was encased in a steel cylinder twenty feet long and nearly seven feet in diameter, along with a fission-type bomb that would explode first, causing the deuterium to go critical. This was the so-called two-stage design developed by Teller and Ulam. The explosion would take place on an island named Elugelab at the U.S.

test range on the Pacific atoll Eniwetok. Located some three thousand miles west of Hawaii, Eniwetok had already been the site of several atomic bomb tests after the war. Now, everything was ready for the superbomb test, which was code-named Mike.

At 7:15 A.M. on November 1, 1952, a radio signal from the ship USS *Estes* detonated the world's first thermonuclear explosion. The entire island of Elugelab disappeared, replaced by a crater 164 feet deep and more than a mile across. The bomb's mushroom cloud rose to over 100,000 feet in altitude and spread to more than one hundred miles in diameter. Measurements showed that the Mike explosion was equivalent to 10.4 megatons of TNT—more than five hundred times more powerful than Little Boy. Scientist George Cowan recalled his reaction to the blast: "I was stunned. I mean, it was

The two-staged deuterium bomb developed by Edward Teller and Stanislaw Ulam explodes on the Eniwetok Atoll in the Pacific.

big. . . . The thing was enormous, bigger than I'd ever imagined it would be. It looked as though it blotted out the whole horizon, and I was standing on the deck of the *Estes,* thirty miles away."[28]

Five thousand miles away, at the University of California at Berkeley, Edward Teller sat in a darkened basement room staring at a tiny point of light on a seismograph. The spot would move when the shock wave from the Mike test reached Berkeley. As Teller recalls, "At last the time signal came that had to be followed by the explosion's shock, and there it seemed to be: The spot of light danced wildly and irregularly. . . . Our first hydrogen bomb had been a success."[29]

Delivering the H-Bomb

For all its success, however, the device exploded that day could not really be called a bomb. Weighing eighty-two tons and filled with liquid deuterium that had to be kept cold, the Mike device could never be loaded into an airplane for release over an enemy target. On March 1, 1954, the United States tested its first deliverable thermonuclear weapon. The test, code-named Castle Bravo, detonated a bomb filled with lithium deuteride, a dry nuclear fuel. The resulting fifteen-megaton explosion exceeded all predictions and was the largest thermonuclear device ever tested by the United States. In 1956 the United States dropped its first H-bomb from a B-52 bomber in a test called Cherokee.

The Soviets countered with their own superbombs. On August 12, 1953, the Soviet Union tested an early version of a thermonuclear device at the Semipalatinsk test site. Nicknamed "Joe 4" (for Joseph Stalin) by the United States, the explosion yielded an energy of four hundred kilotons of TNT. In October 1955, a two-stage superbomb similar to America's Teller-Ulam design was test-dropped from a Soviet bomber. Physicist Andrei Sakharov, the designer of the bomb, called the blast of 1.6 megatons a "magical spectacle."[30] Later, however, Sakharov began having second thoughts about his creation, fearing that "this newly released force could slip out of control and lead to unimaginable disasters."[31] In the 1980s, Sakharov would spend six years in exile for criticizing the Soviet government.

Developing a Nuclear Strategy: Massive Retaliation

Along with the development of nuclear weapons came the need to formulate a strategy for how those weapons would be used in a war. In June 1950 Soviet-backed North Korean troops invaded South Korea, beginning the Korean War. President Truman ordered an immediate expansion of U.S. military strength to help prevent the spread of communism. Although Truman's supreme commander in Korea, General Douglas MacArthur, advocated the use of atomic weapons, the president would not authorize the use of the atomic bomb in the war.

After the Korean War ended in 1953, newly elected president Dwight D. Eisenhower decided that maintaining the conventional forces built up during the Truman administration was becoming too expensive for the United States. To bal-

President Dwight Eisenhower developed a new program called "New Look" that relied on nuclear weapons.

ance the military budget, Eisenhower developed a program called the "New Look," which relied more on nuclear weapons and less on conventional forces (ground troops, tanks, and other non-nuclear forces). Under the New Look, the Strategic Air Command began building up its bomber force, and research and development for a new kind of nuclear delivery vehicle, the ballistic missile, increased.

To go along with the New Look, in 1954 Eisenhower's secretary of state John Foster Dulles developed the concept of "massive retaliation." An integral part of deterrence, massive retaliation meant that Soviet aggression anywhere in the world would result in the United States launching an all-out nuclear attack against the Soviet Union. Thus, even a relatively minor skirmish started by the Soviets could trigger a U.S. nuclear reaction that would obliterate the Soviet Union. There is some question as to whether this doctrine would actually have been used or if it was meant to be just a threat hanging over the Soviet Union. Either way, massive retaliation remained U.S. military policy throughout the 1950s.

Developing a Nuclear Strategy: Flexible Response

With the Soviet Union steadily building up its nuclear weapons arsenal, and with a new president in the White House, the policy of massive retaliation began to fall out of favor in the 1960s. President John F. Kennedy saw that the old policy gave him no options for responding appropriately to the growing possibility of Soviet military adventurism, either conventional or nuclear, around the world. So the idea of "flexible response" was born. Under flexible response, massive retaliation was still an option but to be used only as a last resort. Depending on the type and magnitude of the Soviet aggression, other options would be considered first, ranging from a limited response with conventional forces to all-out nuclear war. Closely associated with the policy of flexible response were two possible attack scenarios: counterforce and countervalue.

A counterforce attack is one directed specifically toward an enemy's military installations. The opponent's ability to stage a counterattack is eliminated while the majority of the civilian population

President John F. Kennedy kept his options open by following a flexible response policy.

is spared, thus resulting in a "limited" nuclear war that ends without the total annihilation of the combatants. Counterforce was made an official U.S. policy in 1962. Countervalue strikes, on the other hand, target an enemy's population centers, resulting in loss of civilian life and destruction of property on a massive scale. The threat of a countervalue attack is a strong deterrent against a nation considering a first strike against the United States. Policy makers argued that the Soviet Union would recall Japan's surrender following countervalue strikes on Hiroshima and Nagasaki and be deterred from risking that kind of attack on its own cities.

In the United States, the men and aircraft of the Strategic Air Command stood ready to prevent Sakharov's "unimaginable disasters" from happening. But the airplane's primary role as peacekeeper was about to be challenged by a developing technology that would bring the Cold War to the edge of outer space.

Chapter 3

The Arms Race on the Ground: Ballistic Missiles

The first atomic bombs were so big and so heavy that only the largest bombers could carry them. But as atomic technology advanced in the late 1950s, nuclear payloads began to grow lighter and more compact. As a result, military leaders could begin to think about other, more efficient ways to deliver their lethal nuclear warheads. The most promising technology for this purpose was the ballistic missile. These missiles changed the face of the Cold War forever, prompting an escalating arms race that sometimes threatened to spiral out of control.

The First Ballistic Missile

Scientists interested in space travel began experimenting with rockets in the early twentieth century. Before then, all rockets used solid fuel, a propellant that was at best unpredictable. In 1903 Konstantin Tsiolkovsky, a Russian, suggested the use of liquid fuel for rockets. American rocket pioneer Dr. Robert H. Goddard launched the first liquid-fueled rocket in 1926. The next year the German Society for Space Travel was organized in Berlin to study the possibility of space flight. Among the members of the society was a young man named Wernher von Braun.

Born in 1912 in Wirsitz, Germany, von Braun became interested in space at an early age. He began experimenting with liquid-fueled rockets when he was still a university engineering student. Then in 1932 Colonel Walter Dornberger, the head of Adolf Hitler's rocket research program, hired von Braun to design missiles for the German army.

Von Braun began working first at a facility in a suburb of Berlin and then at a new rocket test site at Peenemünde on the Baltic coast. It was at Peenemünde that von Braun and his team developed the V-2, "Vengeance Weapon No. 2." The forty-six-foot-long missile was designed to carry a two-thousand-pound warhead to a

Wernher von Braun holds a model of the V-2 rocket.

More than five hundred V-2s rained down on London and surrounding areas over the next six months. These raids created psychological terror as well as physical destruction, because at the time there was no way to defend against a ballistic missile. (Only later would antiballistic missile systems be developed by the United States and the Soviet Union.) Indeed, the people in targeted areas could not even hear a V-2 coming, for it flew at supersonic speed, arriving at the target before the sound of its rocket engine could be heard.

As a useful weapon, the V-2 came too late in World War II to make a difference to Nazi Germany's defeat. But it was the first blow in a new form of warfare that would ultimately rely on rockets instead of airplanes to deliver the Cold War superpower's deadly nuclear payloads.

target some 150 to 200 miles away—naturally, Germany's enemy Great Britain. Propelled by a liquid-fuel rocket engine, the missile was launched from a mobile platform that could be moved to avoid detection by aerial reconnaissance. After launch, the V-2 flew in a high arcing, or ballistic, trajectory to its target, thus giving a name to this new class of weapon.

From Peenemünde to White Sands

As the war in Europe drew to a close, Wernher von Braun and important members of his rocket research group surrendered to American forces as they advanced through Germany. The most brilliant minds in missile design would become the core of the U.S. postwar rocket program. At about the same time, the Russian army captured Peenemünde, only to find the facility destroyed by Allied bombs. The Soviets eventually managed to round up "hundreds of German workers, technicians, and second-rate scientists."[32] But the United States clearly had gotten the cream of the crop.

Soviet dictator Joseph Stalin was furious. "We defeated Nazi armies; we occupied Berlin and Peenemünde, but the Americans got the rocket engineers. What could be more revolting and more in-

The V-2 missile, a rocket that could carry a five-thousand-pound nuclear warhead, is assembled.

excusable?"[33] Stalin would have been even more enraged to learn that the United States had also obtained enough parts to build one hundred V-2s, shipping them to the U.S. rocket research range at White Sands, New Mexico.

At the White Sands Proving Ground, von Braun and his team assembled V-2s and helped American scientists learn how to build and launch rockets. Between 1946 and 1952 sixty-four V-2s left the launch pads at White Sands. Von Braun gained much valuable knowledge in his progress toward the ultimate goal of space travel. But the U.S. Army wanted him to develop missiles for military purposes. In 1949 von Braun and his team were transferred to the Redstone Arsenal at Huntsville, Alabama, to work on ballistic missiles for the army.

Building the Missiles

Based on their experience in the V-2 program at White Sands, the German team designed a liquid-fueled missile known as the Redstone. The Redstone, named for the facility where it was designed, could carry a five-thousand-pound nuclear warhead a distance of about two hundred miles. It was essentially an American version of Hitler's V-2, and it made its first flight in 1953. But with its relatively short two-hundred-mile and limited payload capacity, the United States still lacked a long-range strategic missile. That need would soon be met by a rocket known as Atlas.

The Atlas would become America's first intercontinental ballistic missile (ICBM). But it almost did not get built. Defense budget cuts in the years after World War II slowed the U.S. missile program almost to a standstill. Americans were more interested in returning to a peacetime economy than in worrying about this new conflict called the Cold War. In addition, there was bitter rivalry among the army, navy, and air force concerning which service should have control over missile development and deployment. All

America's first intercontinental ballistic missile, the Atlas, is built on an assembly line in San Diego, California.

this changed, however, when the Korean War broke out in June 1950. The United States was once again involved in a "hot" war on foreign soil, and this time the enemy was the North Koreans backed by Soviet arms and equipment. Suddenly, funding became available for military projects, including the Atlas. "There has never been a missile like Atlas," commented

Aviation Week magazine in 1955. "Big vehicles have been built before . . . but most big structures have been based on progressive experience with smaller ones. Atlas is the first and has very little to draw on but engineering courage."[34]

The Atlas was originally designed as a huge missile with five rocket engines that developed more than 650,000 pounds of thrust. Such power was necessary to boost the massive nuclear bombs available in the early 1950s. As nuclear weapons became smaller after the Castle Bravo test in 1954, however, the Atlas was redesigned several times, resulting in a smaller but still formidable weapon. The redesigned Atlas stood eighty-five feet tall on its launching pad and was ten feet in diameter. To save weight, it had no internal support structure; instead, it relied on pressurization to keep its thin stainless steel skin in the proper "rocket" shape. The Atlas's three huge rocket engines generated 360,000 pounds of thrust, a force equal to almost two hundred B-36 bombers. Such massive power could boost a nuclear warhead more than six thousand miles to its target. An Atlas launched from the American Midwest, for example, could easily hit Moscow.

In September 1959 the Atlas ICBM became an operational part of the Strategic Air Command's arsenal. By the early 1960s, most were deployed in underground silos scattered across Kansas, Nebraska, Oklahoma, and other midwestern and western states. The silos were concrete bunkers designed to store the Atlas missiles vertically underground to protect them from weather and enemy attack. In an alert, the Atlas would be raised to the surface, filled with fuel, and then fired toward its predetermined target.

In 1955 U.S. intelligence reports revealed that the Soviets had also been working on an ICBM to launch their own newly developed nuclear bombs. Their missile's designer was an engineer named Sergei Korolev.

Korolev's Missile

Sergei Korolev was to the Soviet rocket program what Wernher von Braun was to America's missile effort. Born in 1906, Korolev received a degree in aeronautical engineering in 1929. Like von Braun, Korolev was fascinated with rockets and space travel; he became head of the Soviet Scientific Rocket Research Institute in 1933. After World War II, Korolev and the few German scientists the Soviet Union had managed to acquire began working to build their own version of the V-2. In 1947 Soviet dictator Joseph Stalin, disturbed by the U.S. buildup of strategic bombers with nuclear payloads, gave the order to accelerate the development of an intercontinental missile that could reach America. "Do you realize," Stalin said, "the tremendous strategic importance of machines of this sort? They could be an effective straitjacket for that noisy shopkeeper Harry Truman. . . . The problem of the creation of transatlantic

Sergei Korolev, head of the Soviet Scientific Rocket Research Institute, created the R-7, a three-ton nuclear warhead.

[intercontinental] rockets is of extreme importance to us."[35] With the detonation of its first atomic bomb in 1949, the Soviet Union joined the nuclear arms race as well as the race for an intercontinental delivery system.

Stalin died in 1953, but his intercontinental ballistic missile program lived on under Nikita Khrushchev, who soon as-

cended to power. Korolev impressed Khrushchev with his "unlimited energy and determination . . . a brilliant organizer."[36] Korolev's ICBM, designated R-7, was designed to carry a three-ton nuclear warhead a distance of five thousand miles. The R-7 stood one hundred feet tall and weighed nearly three hundred tons in its launch configuration. A central sustainer core and four huge strap-on boosters combined to create more than 1 million pounds of thrust, a force necessary to lift the gigantic missile off its launcher.

In 1957 the R-7 missile design was ready for a test launch. The first test resulted in a spectacular explosion on the launch pad. Between May and July 1957, five more R-7s were tested, and all failed. Finally, a successful launch of the R-7 was made in August from the Baikonur launch complex near the town of Tyuratam in the Kazakh Republic (now Kazakhstan). The missile followed its planned ballistic trajectory toward the Pacific Ocean, releasing a dummy warhead that burned up upon reentering the atmosphere.

The Soviet propaganda machine wasted no time in proclaiming the success of the R-7. In a boastful announcement, the Soviets declared,

A super-long-distance intercontinental multi-stage ballistic rocket was launched a few days ago. The tests of the rocket were successful. They fully confirmed the correctness of the calculations and the selected design. The rocket flew at a very high, unprecedented altitude. Covering a huge distance in a brief time the rocket landed in the target area. The results obtained show that it was possible to direct rockets to any part of the world.[37]

The announcement was all but ignored, however, by an American public, government, and military establishment that dismissed it as Russian bluster.

American Missiles

Shortly after the Soviets successfully orbited the world's first artificial satellite in October 1957, Premier Khrushchev announced that the Soviet Union would in the future rely on the ICBM for its national defense. "The age of the bomber is over," he said, "you might as well throw them on the fire."[38] The United States already had more long-range nuclear bombers than the Soviet Union, but now President Eisenhower vowed to add missile power to the Strategic Air Command's arsenal. In fact, several missiles were already in the works.

Developed along with the Atlas, the Titan I was a first-generation ICBM. Deployed from 1962 to 1966, this missile had a range of over six thousand miles. Titan I missiles were stored in under-ground silos but had to be raised by elevator to the surface and filled with fuel before they could be launched. This meant a delay of some fifteen minutes before a Titan could be fired, which was a long time if Soviet missiles were heading toward the United States. This problem was remedied by the newer Titan II, which was stored with fuel already on board and could be fired from within the silo. The first of fifty-four Titan II ICBMs, which replaced the Atlas and Titan I, was deployed in 1963 and remained operational until 1967.

The Minuteman missile was the Strategic Air Command's first solid-fuel missile. Using solid fuel allowed a simpler, more economical design by doing away with the piping, pumps, and other equipment required by liquid fuel. The Minuteman I could boost a nuclear payload more than six thousand miles. More than eight hundred of these ICBMs were installed in silos between 1962 and 1966. They were later replaced by the more advanced Minuteman II and Minuteman III missiles, the latter capable of carrying several nuclear warheads. These multiple independently targeted reentry vehicles, or MIRVs, could each be programmed to hit a different target, thus allowing a single Minuteman to strike multiple targets.

Perhaps the most controversial missile of the SAC arsenal was the Missile-X (MX), more commonly known as the Peacekeeper. The MX was over seventy feet tall and, with three solid-fuel stages

The Red Moon

The world's first artificial satellite was launched into orbit from the Baikonur complex on October 4, 1957. This new heavenly object, named *Sputnik* (meaning "fellow traveler" in Russian), was about twenty-two inches in diameter and weighed 184 pounds. It circled the earth every ninety-six minutes at altitudes reaching almost six hundred miles above the earth. Sergei Korolev had designed the sphere, commenting that his device would forever symbolize the dawn of the space age. For America, that sentiment was painfully true. The shiny aluminum *Sputnik* carried two radio transmitters that emitted faint beeps to the earth below. They were a nagging reminder that the Soviet Union had beaten the United States into space.

Americans' reaction to *Sputnik* was swift . . . and they were not at all pleased. *Time* magazine reported on the "Red Moon over the U.S." and the *New York Herald-Tribune* called it "a grave defeat." Texas senator Lyndon Johnson, quoted by Roger D. Launius in the official NASA website (www.hq.nasa.gov), recalled looking up at a sky that now "seemed almost alien. I also remember the profound shock of realizing that it might be possible for another nation to achieve technological superiority over this great country of ours." Ordinary people were afraid that *Sputnik* was a spy satellite, taking pictures and mapping the United States as it passed overhead. They also feared that future satellites could drop hydrogen bombs on America. Many blamed President Dwight D. Eisenhower for allowing the United States to fall so far behind the Soviet Union in technology.

American pride was somewhat restored when a Jupiter C rocket (a modified Redstone) orbited *Explorer*, the first U.S. satellite, on January 31, 1958. It was a small beginning for the space race, but the ballistic missile race was already shifting into high gear.

Sputnik, *the world's first artificial satellite.*

and one liquid-fuel stage, could carry ten nuclear warheads to an enemy more than six thousand miles away. A sophisticated computer guidance system directed the Peacekeeper's warheads to impact within one thousand feet of their targets. The costly MX was designed to take the place of the Minuteman at a time when U.S. missile vulnerability was being questioned by government and military analysts.

During the 1970s, the growth of the Soviet nuclear arsenal alarmed the U.S. military establishment. Not only were absolute numbers of Soviet ICBMs rising dramatically but the missiles were becoming more sophisticated, capable of striking U.S. missile silos with greater accuracy. The MX missile was designed in response, and several new methods for its deployment were considered. According to one plan, called "closely spaced basing," several missile silos would be grouped together in a tightly spaced cluster. Theoretically, an incoming Soviet ICBM might destroy some of the silos, but the debris from the first explosion would disable further incoming

missiles, thus leaving the remaining silos ready to launch a counterattack. Another idea, known as the "racetrack" or "shell game," would shuttle Peacekeeper missiles along roads between several hundred protective shelters. This tactic, it was

Hidden deep underground, the Titan II could carry many nuclear warheads and be targeted to reach multiple sites.

The Missile Gap

By 1958 there was talk in Washington that the United States was falling behind the Soviets in the development and production of nuclear missiles. This "missile gap" was putting the United States at risk of a nuclear first strike; the Soviet Union could launch a massive nuclear attack on the United States before it had a chance to fire its missiles in response. The notion of a missile gap was, at least in part, the result of a 1957 report that said the United States would be vulnerable to a surprise Soviet attack in as little as two years. The report recommended a massive and expensive buildup of U.S. military might.

The missile gap soon became a political issue. Democratic senator Stuart Symington wrote a letter to President Eisenhower expressing his concern over the missile gap. Years before, Symington had also warned Eisenhower about a supposed "bomber gap" between the United States and the Soviet Union. Eisenhower was criticized for not spending enough money to protect America. (During the 1960 presidential campaign, Democratic candidate John F. Kennedy would talk about the missile gap as he campaigned against Richard M. Nixon, who had been Eisenhower's vice president.)

But Eisenhower knew something that he could not divulge: that there was in fact no missile gap. For several years, U.S. spy planes had been making top-secret flights over the Soviet Union, photographing military installations. These secret spy photos showed no evidence of a massive Soviet missile buildup. Indeed, Eisenhower wrote in his book *The White House Years: Waging Peace, 1956–1961* that in 1961 "news out of the Pentagon indicated that the latest intelligence estimates gave the United States nearly a two to one lead over the Soviet Union in combat-ready ICBMs." The missile gap, imaginary as it was, had quietly closed.

argued, would foil an enemy attack because the Soviets would never know exactly where the missiles were. A similar proposal envisioned mounting the MX missiles on railroad cars that would travel along the nation's rail lines in times of crisis, their mobility again making them difficult for the enemy to target.

These and many other suggested deployment schemes were debated by Congress and the military. All were rejected as unacceptably expensive, dubiously effective, or excessively risky to the American public. The air force, for its part, claimed that existing missile silos were not as vulnerable as some believed. Finally, after years of sometimes heated debate, in 1988 fifty MX missiles were loaded into Minuteman silos and the older missiles retired from service.

As the United States was building up its missile arsenal, the Soviet Union was keeping pace with a weapons program of its own.

The Soviet Threat

Although it was a success as a space launch vehicle, the Soviet R-7 (designated the SS-6 Sapwood by the Western powers) was obsolete as a weapon even before it was deployed in 1960. Only four of the missiles were ever placed into service. But Soviet engineers soon came up with other missiles that threatened to tip the balance of power of the Cold War in their favor.

The SS-7 Saddler missile was the first Soviet ICBM to pose a credible threat to the United States. Designed between 1958 and 1961, the SS-7 used storable liquid fuel and could be launched from surface launchers or underground silos. Its range of more than seven thousand miles gave the SS-7 the capability of delivering its nuclear warhead to targets in the United States. However, the SS-7 was not very accurate and could miss its target by more than 1.7 miles. The Soviets deployed 186 Saddlers from 1961 until the missile was phased out beginning in 1971.

The Soviet Union's counterpart to the U.S. Minuteman missile was the SS-11 Sego. More than one thousand SS-11s were deployed between 1966 and 1989 as the Soviet Union raced to catch up with America's growing nuclear arsenal. The SS-11 was powered by liquid-fuel engines and could be launched from a silo in as little as three minutes. The Sego underwent several modifications, and when the latest version was deployed in 1972, it could carry multiple nuclear warheads a distance of sixty-five hundred miles—and with much more accuracy than the SS-7.

The largest ICBM ever deployed by either superpower was the Soviet's SS-18, a missile given the ominous designation "Satan." This one-hundred-foot-tall giant had a launch weight of 465,000 pounds and was boosted aloft in two stages by liquid-fueled engines. The various versions of the SS-18 could carry either a single twenty-megaton warhead or ten 500-kiloton MIRVs. More than three hundred Satans were deployed in silos after entering the Soviet missile arsenal in 1975.

Many other Soviet missiles were designed and tested during the Cold War. But American intelligence agencies and other observers found it difficult to tell whether a Soviet missile was actually deployed or operational. Every year on May 1 the Soviets put on a great May Day parade, rolling their latest weapons in a traditional display of military strength through the streets of Moscow for the Russian public, and the world, to see. Though missiles were always a part of this parade, it was impossible to tell if they were real or merely dummies made for propaganda purposes. Whether they were real or not, however, the presence of Soviet ICBMs had the United States once more questioning the balance of power and rushing to ensure U.S. superiority.

Arming NATO: Intermediate Range Ballistic Missiles

In April 1949 the United States and Canada had joined ten Western European nations to form a mutual defense organization called the North Atlantic Treaty Organization, or NATO. (The Soviet Union would form its own alliance, called the Warsaw Pact, with seven Communist Eastern European nations in 1955.)

The Soviet Union parades an intermediate range ballistic missile across Red Square.

It was the first time in its history that the United States had entered into a peacetime military alliance, and it signaled a U.S. commitment to help protect the free nations of Western Europe from a Soviet invasion. Part of that commitment meant supplying weapons, both conventional and nuclear, to NATO forces. Because of Western Europe's close proximity to the Soviet Union and Soviet satellites in the Communist Eastern bloc, long-range strategic ICBMs were not necessary to defend the NATO nations. For this purpose, shorter-range weapons called theater nuclear weapons were developed. Theater nuclear weapons are so named because they are designed to be used in a particular geographical area, or theater of operation. During the Cold War, Europe became a major theater of operation in the struggle between the United States and the Soviet Union.

According to U.S. intelligence reports, in the early 1950s the Soviet Union was building up an arsenal of intermediate range ballistic missiles (IRBMs). These IRBMs had a range of up to thirty-five hundred miles, less than that of intercontinental ballistic missiles but enough to pose a threat to the free nations of Western Europe. Responding to this Soviet threat, in 1955 President Eisenhower ordered a step-up in the design and production of U.S. IRBMs. One such IRBM under development was the Thor, a liquid-fueled, single-stage missile. The Thor carried a nuclear warhead and had a range of about seventeen hundred miles. The missile could be readied for launch in as little as fifteen minutes.

In June 1959 the first Thor IRBM squadron became operational in the United Kingdom. Although the squadron was officially part of the British Royal Air Force, the U.S. Strategic Air Command trained the British missile crews and maintained and supervised the deployment of the Thor's nuclear warheads. By 1960 four Thor IRBM systems were operational in the United Kingdom. Thor IRBMs were also deployed in Italy and Turkey. In 1964 a new IRBM, the Pershing, was deployed in Germany, and in 1979 an advanced version of this missile, the Pershing II, was approved by NATO for basing in Europe. These missiles, all aimed at the Soviet Union, provided a U.S. nuclear presence in Europe and demonstrated to the Soviet Union that the United States was serious about protecting its NATO allies.

Cruise Missiles

Cruise missiles also played a part in defending Europe, beginning in 1983. A cruise missile is basically a small, pilotless airplane powered by a turbojet engine and carrying either a conventional or nuclear warhead. An advanced computer guidance system and radar control allows the cruise missile to fly low, "hugging" the terrain and maneuvering around obstacles as it makes its way to the target. Although cruise missiles are relatively slow, they can fly below the beams of enemy radar, thus making them difficult to detect. They can conveniently be launched from the ground, from aircraft, and from ships or submarines, which makes the cruise missile an extremely versatile weapon.

At the beginning of the 1960s, faced with all these various weapons systems, neither superpower knew exactly how many weapons the other had, so the arms race became a game of guessing and one-upmanship. Kennedy, who defeated Republican Richard Nixon in the 1960 presidential election, later acknowledged that the superpowers were "caught up in a vicious and dangerous cycle in which suspicion on one side breeds suspicion on the other, and new weapons beget counter-weapons."[39] But no one seemed to know how to end the game.

The Cuban Missile Crisis

In October 1962 that game nearly came to a disastrous conclusion when the United States discovered that the Soviet Union was beginning to install nuclear missiles in Cuba. Aerial reconnaissance

Atomic Weapons on the Battlefield

The most destructive weapons of the Cold War were certainly the intercontinental ballistic missiles that could hurl nuclear warheads thousands of miles onto the enemy homeland. But what about the ordinary soldier on the battlefield? Was he limited to old-fashioned guns and conventional explosives in the age of atomic power? In fact, many nuclear weapons were designed for tactical, or battlefield, use to supplement the strategic role played by the ICBMs. Many "battlefield nukes" were developed to help NATO forces defend Europe and counter possible Soviet expansion in the region. During the Eisenhower administration, nuclear cannon shells, short-range missiles, and even nuclear land mines were developed. One general estimated that the army needed more than 100,000 battlefield nuclear weapons, stating that 423 nuclear warheads might be used in *one day's* combat. This was at a time when the total U.S. nuclear stockpile contained less than seven thousand weapons.

One tactical nuclear weapon was the Davy Crockett, a nuclear-tipped projectile designed to be fired from a special recoilless rifle mounted on a jeep or carried and fired by a three-man crew. The Davy Crockett was the smallest nuclear weapon ever deployed by the United States and was able to deliver its fifty-one-pound nuclear warhead to targets up to two and a half miles away. The nuclear yield of the Davy Crockett's M54 warhead ranged from .01 to 1 kiloton of TNT. Beginning in 1961, about twenty-one hundred Davy Crocketts were put into service by the U.S. Army at a cost of $540 million. (The cost of the warheads was extra.)

As it turned out, however, tests showed that the Davy Crockett was too inaccurate to be of much use in actual combat, and it was removed from service in 1971. In addition, there was never any clear plan on how to use such weapons on the battlefield. Army captain John J. Midgley commented in a report called "The Atomic Audit," which can be found on the *Bulletin of Atomic Scientists* website (www. bullatomsci.org),

> The technical characteristics of systems developed in the late 1950s and early 1960s— particularly the Davy Crockett—exerted relentless pressure toward a strategy which relied on widespread, decentralized nuclear operations. . . . The nuclear battlefield remained an ill-defined and little understood environment, useful as a justification for equipment and weapon procurement but not considered as a basis for force design.

U.S. Army soldiers operate a Davy Crockett missile.

photos clearly showed missiles and missile launchers on the island located just ninety miles off the Florida coast. Once operational, the missiles could have hit numerous population centers in the southeastern United States. During the tense two-week standoff that ensued, some U.S. military leaders advocated a nuclear first strike against the Soviet Union. The crisis finally ended peacefully through negotiations, and the Soviet missiles were removed from Cuba.

The Cuban Missile Crisis brought the world the closest it has ever been to all-out nuclear war. And it shocked the two superpowers into realizing that there would be no winner in a nuclear war: A first strike would bring a counterstrike, and both sides would be destroyed. They also were beginning to recognize the danger that radioactive fallout posed to the world. Since the beginning of the arms race, both the United States and the Soviet Union, in their quest for ever more powerful nuclear weapons, had been performing atmospheric and underground nuclear tests. The concern that fallout from above-ground tests could contaminate

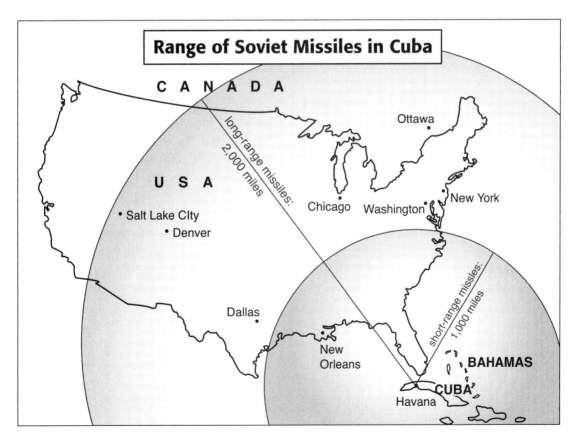

Range of Soviet Missiles in Cuba

the air, soil, and water far from the test site led to an informal ban on these tests. The year after the Cuban Missile Crisis, that moratorium was made official.

Slowing the Race

In August 1963 the United States and the Soviet Union (along with Great Britain, which was also performing nuclear tests) signed the Partial Test Ban Treaty. This treaty, sometimes called the Limited Test Ban Treaty, forbade the testing of nuclear weapons in the atmosphere, in space, or under the ocean. Underground testing, where fallout could be controlled, was not prohibited by the treaty, and the Soviet Union and the United States both continued to carry out underground testing.

Along with an official treaty comes the need for "verification" to determine if both sides are in compliance with the terms of that treaty. The Soviet Union's position on verification of the Partial Test Ban Treaty differed from that of the United States. The American position demanded on-site inspections in which teams of inspectors would personally visit arsenals in the Soviet Union to make sure the treaty terms were in force. The Soviets, on the other hand, considered this simply another way that America could spy on them, and thus declared on-site inspections unacceptable. Instead, they insisted that current "national technical means of verification" were sufficient to detect any breaches of the treaty without the necessity of inspectors on Soviet soil.

Such verification methods included satellite photography, seismographs to keep track of underground blasts, and airborne radiation and air pressure sensors to warn of any illegal atmospheric tests. Verification and on-site inspection would be a constant sticking point in future arms negotiations between the United States and the Soviet Union.

In calling on the American people to support the Partial Test Ban Treaty, Kennedy had said the treaty "would place the nuclear powers in a position to deal more effectively with one of the greatest hazards that man faces in 1963, the further spread of nuclear arms."[40] Still, nuclear stockpiles continued to grow.

Stockpiles and SIOP

As the U.S. nuclear arsenal grew, the logistics of deploying and stockpiling weapons soon became increasingly difficult. Each branch of the armed forces had its own nuclear inventory and its own policies for targeting bombs and warheads. A plan was needed to integrate U.S. nuclear forces, and in 1960 the Single Integrated Operational Plan (SIOP) was devised. SIOP was (and is, since it is still in effect) the U.S. plan for fighting a nuclear war. Initially, several different scenarios were envisioned, ranging from a limited targeting of Soviet strategic forces (military airfields and missile launch sites) to allout nuclear destruction of the Soviet Union. The top-secret plan coordinates the employment of nuclear weapons in

Explosion at Silo 7

During the Cold War, hundreds of ICBMs waited in their underground silos, fueled and ready for the firing order that everyone hoped would never come. The possibility of a nuclear accident was never very far from the minds of the residents of towns and farms near the missile silos. In September 1980 just such an accident occurred near the town of Damascus, Arkansas. The following account of a mishap in a Titan II silo is quoted in *The Nuclear Almanac: Confronting the Atom in War and Peace*, compiled by faculty members at the Massachusetts Institute of Technology:

> Eight maintenance men were pressurizing the oxidizer tank, a routine procedure. One man dropped a wrench socket at about 6:30 P.M. . . . which fell about seventy feet, bounced off a mounting, and punched a three- to five-inch break in the metal skin of the fuel tank. The leaking fuel triggered an automatic safety system which sprayed water on the rocket to dissolve the fuel and carry it to a cavity below the missile. The system was not designed to handle fuel leaks as large as this one, however, and fuel vapors continued to enter the air in the missile silo. . . . Before dawn on September 19, 1980 a violent explosion rent the Titan II missile silo near Damascus, Arkansas. There was a tremendous wind blast and fireball. Large steel fragments flew into the sky as the force blew off the 740-ton silo cover. The silo and missile were destroyed—the nine-megaton nuclear warhead fell to the ground some 200 yards from the silo. . . . The violent explosion occurred shortly after a team of two airmen had been ordered to reenter the evacuated silo to determine whether the concentration of fuel vapors had subsided. One of the airmen was killed; his partner and twenty others were injured.

Fortunately, the nuclear warhead did not detonate, and although several nearby towns were evacuated, there was no radioactive contamination of the area where it fell. This was not the worst Titan II accident, however. On August 9, 1965, fifty-three men were killed when a fire raged through a silo in Searcy, Arkansas. The U.S. Air Force has said that there were 125 accidents at Titan missile silos between 1975 and 1979.

all the military branches and plays a key role in U.S. nuclear policy and foreign affairs. Each year, the SIOP is reviewed and updated to reflect the current world situation.

The United States now had a plan for using nuclear weapons, and it had the weapons to use. America's nuclear stockpile reached its peak in 1966, with more than thirty-two thousand nuclear warheads and bombs either deployed or in reserve. The Soviet Union had about seven thousand nuclear weapons, far fewer than the United States but still enough to destroy the nation. This number was merely an estimate on the part of U.S. officials, however, for there was no way to precisely determine the true number of Soviet warheads. Both sides kept information about their nuclear arsenals as secret as possible, so tallying the enemy's strength was an elaborate guessing game, aided by aerial surveillance information and other types of espionage activity.

The Strategy of MAD

By the late 1960s Great Britain and France had successfully built a few atomic bombs, and China was conducting tests of nuclear devices. But the superpowers had by far the largest nuclear arsenals, and their enormous stockpiles led to the development of a new nuclear strategy known as the doctrine of mutual assured destruction, or, appropriately, MAD. Since each superpower could destroy the other many times over, it would be suicide to start a nuclear war. Some people thought there had to be a better way to avoid a war than by nuclear proliferation, and the Soviet Union never officially adopted the doctrine. But in its ironic way, MAD seemed to work: The very existence of thousands of nuclear weapons may have prevented their use.

Intercontinental ballistic missiles, the second leg of the triad, took nuclear arms to the edges of outer space. Running swiftly and silently, the triad's third leg brought nuclear weapons to the depths of the sea.

Chapter 4

The Arms Race at Sea

Although nuclear energy was the basic force behind the enormous destructive power of the atomic bomb, Cold War scientists knew it could also be used in other, less destructive ways. It could, for example, become a cheap and efficient source of propulsion for many types of vehicles. A nuclear-powered airplane had been tested, with little success. It would take the U.S. Navy to successfully mate nuclear power with a military vehicle. The result was a deadly vessel of war, packing a nuclear punch.

The Nuclear Submarine

Submarines have long played a part in naval history. During the American Revolution, David Bushnell built a submersible named the *Turtle* and attempted to sink a British warship with a gunpowder bomb. The plan failed, as did another attempt during the War of 1812. During the Civil War, the Confederate submarine *Hunley* sank the Union ship *Housatonic* but never returned from its mission. In 1900 the navy commissioned its first modern submarine, the *Holland*, and by the end of World War II some 288 U.S. subs had sunk more than 1,300 Japanese merchant ships, depriving the island nation of vital raw materials needed for their war effort.

As effective as they were, however, these submarines were essentially surface vessels that could operate for limited periods underwater. Propelled by diesel engines on the surface, the subs ran on battery-powered motors while submerged. When its batteries ran low (after only a few hours submerged), a submarine had to surface to recharge them. To overcome this drawback, a new kind of power source was needed, one that did not require air to work or need recharging. To Captain Hyman G. Rickover it seemed that atomic power fit the bill perfectly. Now he just had to convince the U.S. Navy that he was right.

The *Nautilus*

Rickover had commanded only one ship—an old wooden minesweeper—but what he lacked in command experience he made up for in vision. And his vision was a nuclear-powered navy. In 1946 Rickover was assigned to the Manhattan Project's Oak Ridge facility to help develop an atomic power plant that could be used in a submarine. But the navy still had plenty of World War II subs in commission and failed to see the advantages of an atomic-powered boat. Undaunted, Rickover pushed through his ideas using unconventional and often confrontational methods. In 1951 Congress authorized construction of a nuclear-powered submarine; in January 1954, eighteen months after its keel was laid, the USS *Nautilus* was launched with a traditional bottle of champagne broken across its bow. One year later the commissioned vessel was put to work.

Although it resembled an ordinary World War II submarine, what was inside its hull made it a revolutionary naval weapon: The USS *Nautilus* was the first ship to be powered by a nuclear reactor. On January 17, 1955, Commander Eugene Wilkinson began the first operational voyage of the *Nautilus*, signaling the momentous words: "UNDERWAY ON NUCLEAR POWER."[41] As the *Nautilus* headed for the deep waters of the Atlantic Ocean, it marked the beginning of a new era in seagoing warfare.

Submerged, the *Nautilus* could travel at a speed of more than twenty knots (twenty-three miles per hour), a speed unmatched by conventional submarines. And without having to surface to recharge batteries, its range was limited only by the crew's endurance and food supply. In 1958 the *Nautilus* made history by being the first vessel to reach the polar ice cap at the top of the world—the North Pole.

Six torpedo tubes made the *Nautilus* a true attack submarine, designed to seek out and destroy enemy vessels. More advanced attack submarines soon followed. Based on a radical, new design first employed in the 1950s on a submarine named the USS *Albacore*, the new attack subs became more streamlined, employing a teardrop-shaped hull. This new shape allowed for increased speed and maneuverability as well as quieter operation underwater. The *Albacore*-style hull influenced the design of all future U.S. submarines. In 1959 the USS *Skipjack* was commissioned, the first U.S. submarine to incorporate both nuclear propulsion and the new, streamlined hull.

Attack submarines beginning with the USS *Nautilus* represented a new era in naval warfare. "The *Nautilus* is not merely an improved weapon," Rickover commented, "she is the most potent and deadly weapon afloat. She is, in fact, a new weapon."[42] The next step for the navy was to give this new weapon a nuclear punch.

Polaris

When the Soviet Union began its rapid buildup of its intercontinental ballistic

Powered by a nuclear reactor, the USS Nautilus *leaves New York harbor.*

missile arsenal in the late 1950s, the United States began to worry about a pre-emptive nuclear strike, an attack that would destroy U.S. missile sites and leave the United States defenseless. Despite being stored in protective silos, land-based ICBMs were vulnerable to attack because the Soviets knew where they were. But if missiles could be carried aboard and launched from submarines, an enemy would have a difficult time knowing exactly where those weapons were located at any given time. The ability to move around and stay submerged made the nuclear submarine an ideal missile-

launching platform. Now a suitable missile was needed, and Congress funded research on a new design called Polaris.

In 1956 the navy received the go-ahead to build a solid propellant submarine-launched ballistic missile (SLBM). Named Polaris, the missile was twenty-eight feet long, fifty-four inches in diameter, and weighed about twenty-eight thousand pounds. The use of solid rather than liquid fuel in its two stages made the missile safer and easier to store aboard submarines.

Death of a Nuclear Submarine

When the nuclear submarine USS *Thresher* (SSN-593) was launched on July 9, 1960, it was the most advanced attack submarine ever built. It was also the beginning of a tragically short life for the *Thresher* and its crew. The following account of the sinking of the USS *Thresher* was taken from the *Dictionary of American Naval Fighting Ships*, found on the Naval Historical Center website (www.history.navy.mil):

> In company with *Skylark* (ASR-20) [a surface ship assisting the *Thresher*], *Thresher* put to sea on 10 April 1963 for deep-diving exercises. In addition to her 16 officers and 96 enlisted men, the submarine carried 17 civilian technicians to observe her performance during the deep-diving tests. Fifteen minutes after reaching her assigned test depth, the submarine communicated with *Skylark* by underwater telephone, apprising the submarine rescue ship of difficulties. Garbled transmissions indicated that—far below the surface—things were going wrong. Suddenly, listeners in *Skylark* heard a noise "like air rushing into an air tank"— then, silence.
>
> Efforts to reestablish contact with *Thresher* failed, and a search group was formed in an attempt to locate the submarine. Rescue ship *Recovery* (ASR-43) subsequently recovered bits of debris, including gloves and bits of internal insulation. Photographs taken by bathyscaph *Trieste* proved that the submarine had broken up, taking all hands on board to their deaths in 5,500 feet of water, some 220 miles east of Boston. *Thresher* was officially declared lost in April 1963.
>
> Subsequently, a Court of Inquiry was convened and, after studying pictures and other data, opined that the loss of *Thresher* was in all probability due to a casting, piping, or welding failure that flooded the engine room with water. This water probably caused electrical failures that automatically shut down the nuclear reactor, causing an initial power loss and the eventual loss of the boat.

The *Thresher* did not die in vain. After reviewing the disaster, the U.S. Navy modified its standards for the design, construction, and operation of nuclear submarines. The result was a safer nuclear fleet and no repetition of the *Thresher* disaster.

An intermediate range missile, the Polaris could deliver a single five-hundred-kiloton nuclear warhead to a target about twelve hundred miles away. Later versions of the Polaris carried multiple warheads and had a range of more than twenty-five hundred miles.

With the development of the Polaris well under way, the navy began looking for a suitable submarine to carry it. The *Nautilus*, a nuclear attack submarine (designated SSN by the navy), was too small to be fitted with the new missiles. So, a new type of sub, the ballistic missile submarine (SSBN), was developed.

Out of the Deep

Just as the concept of an intercontinental ballistic missile had emerged from the Nazi V-2 rocket, the idea for a missile-carrying submarine had actually originated with Nazi documents captured after World War II. The German navy had experimented with putting mortar tubes on the deck of a U-boat (the German term for submarine) and firing them from the partially submerged sub at land-based targets. The U.S. Navy carried the German idea further, and the result was the world's first ballistic missile submarine, the USS *George Washington*.

The *George Washington* actually began as an attack submarine, the USS *Scorpion*, which was already under construction. But out of fear that the Soviets were also developing missile subs, President Eisenhower gave the highest priority to the building of U.S. SSBNs. The *Scorpion* was split apart and a 130-foot-long section was inserted in the middle of the unfinished hull. This new section contained sixteen tubes designed to carry Polaris missiles, along with the systems to maintain, control, and fire the missiles. The construction of the *George Washington* was completed in record time, less than three years after authorization.

The first underwater test launch of a Polaris missile was made from the *George*

Washington on July 28, 1960. Designers and navy admirals watched the tests with apprehension; previous land-based Polaris tests had been conspicuous failures. John Piña Craven, the chief scientist of the Polaris project, described the launch: "The missile emerges from the water at

A Polaris test missile launches from a submerged submarine.

an atrocious angle in pitch and roll. It appears doomed for failure, but miraculously rights itself and streaks off to its target downrange."[43] A second test missile also performed flawlessly, prompting an admiral to comment, "Out of the deep to target, perfect."[44]

Boomers

On November 15, 1960, the USS *George Washington* began its first operational patrol, armed with sixteen Polaris missiles. The sub was assigned two complete crews—the Blue and Gold crews—of 133 men each. One crew would operate the *George Washington* for a typical two-month tour and then the other crew would take over for the next patrol, keeping the submarine continuously operational. Silently prowling the alien world beneath the ocean, the *George Washington* had the feel of a spacecraft adrift in a vast galactic void. One crewman called the sub a "space station in the sea."[45]

The *George Washington*, armed with its load of Polaris missiles, was the first of a naval weapons system called the Fleet Ballistic Missile system. It was also the first of the "*George Washington* class" of fleet SSBNs. Four other missile subs—the *Patrick Henry*, the *Theodore Roosevelt*, the *Robert E. Lee*, and the *Abraham Lincoln*—joined the *George Washington* in its role as a deterrent to Soviet aggression. Soon, another class of five ballistic missile submarines, the *Ethan Allen* class, would begin construction. In all, the navy planned to build forty-one ballistic missile submarines. Befitting their role as the launch platform for nuclear missiles, the SSBNs were nicknamed "boomers."

While the first boomers were still being built, missile technology was advancing. The Poseidon missile, placed in service in 1971, was larger than the Polaris and could deliver up to fourteen nuclear warheads (although it usually carried only ten) with increased accuracy. In 1979 a new missile named Trident went into operation. Designed as a replacement for the Poseidon, the Trident was a three-stage, solid-fuel missile with a range of more than forty-five hundred miles, twice that of the Poseidon. This increased range allowed a submarine carrying Trident missiles to patrol a larger undersea area and still be able to hit an enemy target. An additional advantage was a new stellar guidance system, which increased the accuracy of the Trident. As this latest generation of submarine-launched ballistic missiles was developed, a new submarine was needed to deploy them.

The USS *Ohio* was the first of a new class of ballistic missile submarines that were larger, carried more missiles, and, most important, were quieter (to prevent detection by an enemy) than any previous SSBN. Measuring some 560 feet long (nearly twice the length of a football field) and forty-two feet wide, the *Ohio* was fitted with twenty-four Trident missiles carrying multiple warheads. The sub's nuclear reactor powered a steam

An Ohio-*class submarine carrying Trident ballistic missiles leaves its port to patrol the Atlantic and Pacific Oceans.*

vember 1981. Nine more *Ohio*-class SSBNs commissioned during the 1980s patrolled both the Atlantic and Pacific Oceans with their complement of deadly Trident missiles. Able to operate for at least fifteen years without an overhaul, each sub spent at least two-thirds of its time at sea. The *Ohio*-class boomers were the mainstay of the U.S. deterrent force under the oceans in the 1980s, the last decade of the Cold War.

In 1948 U.S. Naval Intelligence had estimated that the Soviet Union might be producing submarines at such a rate that within three years it could have one thousand nuclear subs patrolling the oceans. Such estimates helped spur the development of U.S. nuclear attack and missile submarines. But were the Soviets really building submarines so quickly?

turbine that turned a single propeller and could propel the *Ohio* at more than twenty-five knots (more than twenty-eight miles per hour) while submerged.

The *Ohio* was launched in 1979 and commissioned into the U.S. Navy in No-

Soviet Naval Power

During World War II, Soviet submarines and surface vessels were largely ineffective against the German navy. After the war, the Soviet wartime fleet was no match for burgeoning U.S. naval power. Soviet dictator Joseph Stalin had planned to rebuild his navy into a great oceangoing fleet, but with his death in 1953 these plans also died. Soviet military planners

The Jennifer Project

One of the most sought-after goals in the game of naval espionage is the capture of an enemy vessel, complete with its nuclear weapons, code books, and other intelligence information. In 1974 the United States had a chance to do just that, with the help of some fabulous technology, the Central Intelligence Agency, and an eccentric.

On April 11, 1968, a Soviet Golf II–class nuclear missile submarine sank with all hands into 17,000 feet of water some 750 miles northwest of Hawaii in the Pacific Ocean. Although Soviet search vessels could not find the sub, the United States knew where it was; it had been tracking the Golf with underwater listening devices. The U.S. Central Intelligence Agency hatched a plan, code-named the Jennifer Project, to secretly recover the downed submarine. The plan called for sending a vessel built by billionaire Howard Hughes, the *Glomar Explorer*, to attempt the pickup. A cover story was concocted in which Hughes's ship would sail to the Pacific to collect manganese nodules, valuable clumps of minerals, from the ocean floor.

The *Glomar Explorer*, a six-hundred-foot mining ship, was outfitted with special equipment designed to lift the Soviet sub from the bottom. The ship set sail on June 20, 1974, and was soon anchored over the site of the wreck. From the center of the *Glomar Explorer* a long steel pipe with eight giant claws was secretly lowered through more than three miles of ocean to where the Golf rested on the bottom. A miscalculation sent the claws too far, slamming them into the seafloor. But an inspection by video camera showed no damage, so the operation continued.

It took days to descend the 17,000 feet to where the sub lay, fighting the swirling ocean current all the way. Finally reaching the bottom, the claws grasped the submarine and began the trip to the surface at an agonizingly slow rate of six feet per minute. Then disaster struck. Three of the claws gave way and the sub began to break up, the bulk of it falling back to rest forever on the Pacific seabed.

Accounts differ on just what the Jennifer Project accomplished. One story says that only 10 percent of the Golf, with no valuable hardware or information, was retrieved, while other accounts state that missiles and code books were recovered. Whatever the truth is, the Jennifer Project was a daring chapter in the annals of Cold War espionage.

turned to bombers and intercontinental ballistic missiles to counteract the increasing threat posed by the U.S. Strategic Air Command. With most of the limited Soviet military budget going to ICBMs and aircraft, there was very little left for rebuilding the Soviet navy.

Neither this situation nor the legacy of Soviet naval failures, however, discouraged Admiral Sergei G. Gorshkov, the commander-in-chief of the Soviet navy.

Gorshkov recognized the value of submarines as a deterrent to a growing U.S. Navy and pushed for the construction of a modern submarine fleet. The first Soviet postwar attack submarines (designated Zulu class by NATO) were powered by conventional diesel engines and batteries and were partly based on the design of captured German U-boats. The Soviet Union would continue to build these conventionally powered subs throughout the

Cold War. One Zulu-class boat became the first Soviet missile submarine.

Among the documents the Soviets captured from Germany was information about an experimental missile-launching system devised for German submarines. This odd system called for a submarine to tow a V-2 missile behind it in a barge or container. Once at the launch point, the container would be flooded to position it vertically and the V-2 would be fired at a land-based target. The Germans never developed this launching method, but the Soviets tried it in the late 1940s, building several hundred missile containers. The system never worked, however, and was not put into operation. The Soviets did fit a single launch tube on a Zulu-class submarine and loaded an SS-1 "Scud" missile into the tube. On September 16, 1955, the missile was successfully test-fired, nearly five years before the USS *George Washington* launched its first missile. Thus the Soviet Union became the first nation to actually fire a submarine-launched ballistic missile.

By 1959 six Zulu-class submarines were in service, each carrying two SS-1 missiles with conventional warheads. But these missiles were cumbersome to fire and, being liquid fueled, were dangerous to store aboard the subs. Also, with a range of less than one hundred miles, the missiles posed virtually no threat to the United States. Nevertheless, the mere existence of an SLBM system demonstrated that the Soviets were serious about

developing a seaborne missile capability. They were also serious about developing nuclear-powered submarines.

Soviet Nuclear Submarines

The Soviet Union had begun planning for the construction of nuclear submarines in 1952. The first Soviet nuclear submarine, the *K-3*, also called the *Leninsky Komsomol* was launched on September 9, 1957, and entered into service in 1958. All vessels in this first Soviet series were categorized as "November class" (non-U.S.) submarines; this attack submarine had two nuclear reactors and could reach a speed of thirty miles per hour submerged. It carried twenty torpedoes that could be fired from eight torpedo tubes. By 1964, fifty-five nuclear submarines, including thirteen November class, were a part of the Soviet navy. The November-class subs were plagued by problems, however, including reactor accidents such as a radioactive gas leak on the Soviet sub *K-27* in 1968 that killed nine men.

The Soviet Union's counterpart to the USS *George Washington* ballistic missile submarine was the Yankee-class nuclear subs, which began entering the Soviet fleet in 1967. Like the *George Washington*, the Yankee submarines carried sixteen ballistic missiles housed in vertical launch tubes within the hull. The first missiles deployed in the Yankees could deliver a one-megaton warhead to a target some eighteen hundred miles away; later missiles could boost multiple warheads nearly five

A Typhoon-class submarine, designed to function under the polar ice caps, sits in a Soviet harbor.

thousand miles. Further submarine development gave rise to the Delta-class and Typhoon-class submarines. At more than 564 feet long and eighty feet wide, the Typhoons were the largest submarines ever built by any nation. Typhoon-class submarines were designed to sit under the polar ice cap during a nuclear war and then crash through the ice to deliver a retaliatory blow. Their twenty missiles, each carrying up to ten nuclear warheads, made the Typhoons the most feared weapons in the Soviet naval arsenal.

One of the most important aspects of a nuclear submarine's mission is to re-main undetected while on patrol. The challenge for a nation's navy is to try to detect where an enemy submarine is and track its movements. During the Cold War, a deadly serious game of "cat and mouse" was played out in the depths of an unforgiving ocean.

Hide and Seek

As the Soviet Union continued to build up its submarine strength in the post-

World War II years, U.S. intelligence agencies scrambled to find out as much information as they could about the deadly new weapons the Soviets were developing. And it seemed that U.S. submarines were the ideal vessels to acquire that information. During the course of the cold war, U.S. submarines lurked near Soviet harbors, gathering intelligence about onshore activities and tracking the movements of Soviet subs. Above all, it was vital to keep track of the Soviet ballistic missile submarines that could unleash a devastating first strike on the United States, a "nuclear Pearl Harbor" that would catch U.S. defenses off guard.

Submarine espionage began in the late 1940s with diesel-electric submarines. Fitted with sensitive listening devices and passive sonar, the subs were to try to identify and learn as much as they could about Soviet surface vessels. When the first Soviet Yankee-class ballistic missile submarines appeared, priority was given to spying on this new weapon. In 1969 the attack submarine USS *Lapon*, under the command of Chester Mack, photographed a Yankee sub and then, in an amazing feat of underwater stealth espionage, trailed the Yankee undetected for forty-seven days. From then on, trailing Soviet boomers became a top priority for the U.S. Navy, and U.S. sub crews listened for any unusual sounds. "Our submarine in trail," commented a U.S. submarine official, "was always alert to any activity of the Soviet that indicated he was getting ready to launch. Like the opening of the outer doors of the missile tube . . . like flooding the tube, this is a critical indication that he's getting ready to launch."[46]

The Soviets responded to U.S. submarine espionage by undertaking the same kind of spying with their subs. In addition, Soviet trawlers, under the guise of being innocent fishing vessels, were equipped with secret electronic eavesdropping equipment. U.S. submarines took pains to steer clear of these spy ships.

Despite efforts to remain hidden, the close proximity of submarines engaged in spy activities occasionally put hunter and prey on a collision course. Throughout the Cold War many undersea impacts occurred, usually resulting in dented hulls and other repairable damage. Just a few months after the *Lapon*'s forty-seven-day spy odyssey, the U.S. submarine *Gato* bumped a Soviet missile sub, causing minor damage to both subs. In some cases, however, the damage was more serious. In June 1970 a violent crash occurred between the USS *Tautog* and a Soviet missile submarine named *Black Lila* off the coast of the Soviet Union. Initial evidence indicated that the Soviet sub had sunk, but later its commanding officer came forth and confirmed that the *Black Lila* had survived the collision.

U.S. nuclear submarines played an active role in spying on Soviet submarines. But the United States soon began employing another, passive method for underwater espionage.

Underwater Ears

When a Soviet submarine left its port to begin a patrol or returned after a long period at sea, the United States knew within a short time about the vessel's movement. This information was gathered by a network of undersea listening devices called the Sound Surveillance System, or SOSUS. Beginning in the 1950s, lines of hydrophones (sensitive underwater microphones) were placed at strategic points at the bottom of the world's oceans. Lines were established along the coasts of the United States and in the Barents Sea, as well as in the northern Pacific Ocean between Japan and the Aleutian Islands. Hydrophones were also deployed in other areas of the oceans. The SOSUS hydrophones were connected by undersea cables to land installations where sound information was gathered, recorded, and interpreted by acoustic experts. The engine sounds and propeller noise of any Soviet submarine crossing the SOSUS lines would immediately give an indication of the sub's speed, direction, and type.

With U.S. submarines trailing them and listening ears at the bottom of the ocean revealing their movements, Soviet submarines were not as stealthy as their commanders had hoped. Still, they presented a deadly threat of mass destruction. However, the Cold War at sea did not take place only beneath the waves. U.S. Navy surface ships played a highly visible role in the conflict.

Operation Sea Orbit

On May 13, 1964, three U.S. Navy ships embarked on a historic voyage. The vessels—the guided missile cruiser USS *Long Beach*, the guided missile frigate USS *Bainbridge*, and the aircraft carrier USS *Enterprise*—formed a seagoing group called Task Force One. The voyage they were making was a trip around the world called Operation Sea Orbit. What made Operation Sea Orbit important was that the ships would make the entire journey without refueling, for the *Long Beach*, *Bainbridge*, and *Enterprise* were all nuclear-powered vessels.

With the success of the submarine *Nautilus*, it seemed that the nuclear submarine would soon dominate the navy's traditional surface fleet of battleships, destroyers, cruisers, and frigates. Admiral Charles Momsen predicted that the time would come "when the surface Navy will be turned into obsolete hulks by submarines. . . . The entire Navy will have to go underwater. That's where tomorrow's great sea battles will be fought and won."[47] Despite such predictions, however, it soon became clear that the advantages of nuclear power could also be employed by the navy's surface fleet. The USS *Long Beach* began its service as the first nuclear-powered surface ship in September 1961. It was the first cruiser specifically designed to carry missiles instead of guns as its main armament, thus its designation as a guided missile cruiser. The guided missile frigate *Bainbridge* was a smaller

$E=mc^2$

Task Force One aircraft carrier USS Enterprise *embarks on a round-the-world voyage.*

vessel than the *Long Beach*, but its missiles were just as deadly.

Nuclear power was incorporated into aircraft carriers as well. On September 24, 1960, the nuclear-powered carrier USS *Enterprise* was commissioned. The *Enterprise*, whose famous name has been carried on eight U.S. Navy ships since 1775, began its maiden voyage under nuclear propulsion on January 12, 1962. With its eight nuclear reactors, it could reach a speed of more than thirty miles per hour. In October of that year, the *Enterprise* was one of the ships participating in quaran-

tine operations during the Cuban Missile Crisis. Two years later the *Enterprise* and its companion ships of Task Force One completed their around-the-world voyage, having traveled a total of 30,565 miles under nuclear power. The *Enterprise* also has the distinction of being the first nuclear vessel to see combat, when its aircraft carried out raids during the Vietnam War.

With all the deterrent advantages of nuclear submarines, such as their ability to remain undetected as they stand ready to deliver their ballistic missiles, a surface fleet might seem a bit old-fashioned. But the very fact that such ships are highly visible gives them a deterrent factor that cannot be duplicated by submarines hiding deep below the surface.

Forward Presence

In the long history of the U.S. Navy, the use of a display of power, sometimes called "gunboat diplomacy," has been a part of naval strategy. When a dangerous political or military situation threatens American interests overseas, the U.S. Navy can dispatch surface ships to the area as a visible demonstration that the United States is willing to protect its allies and interests around the world. This "forward presence" of U.S. warships near another nation's homeland can make a hostile power think twice about risking an armed confrontation with the United States. Aircraft carriers in particular, with their squadrons of nuclear-armed fighters and bombers ready to strike at targets on land, at sea, or in the air, are a prime component of forward presence.

In 1907 President Theodore Roosevelt sent a fleet of sixteen battleships, called the "Great White Fleet" because of the ships' gleaming white hulls, around the world to showcase U.S. naval power. Operation Sea Orbit in 1964 was another such demonstration, with the addition of nuclear power to reinforce the navy's message that it can, and will, go anywhere in the world. Throughout the Cold War, both superpowers relied on this visible presence to intimidate and deter each other and to prepare themselves should the conflict reach the point of armed confrontation.

Chapter 5

Protecting the Homeland

During World War II, the United States, distanced from enemies Germany and Japan by two huge oceans, remained relatively safe from attack. Even with a few Japanese "balloon bombs" ineffectively launched against the west coast and German submarines patrolling off the eastern seaboard, Americans had little to fear. The Cold War, however, changed that complacent mindset. Nuclear-tipped Soviet ICBMs could now reach the very heartland of America, and U.S. officials had to devise ways of detecting, and averting, this unprecedented threat.

Alert!

June 3, 1980, began as just another routine night for the midnight-shift air and ground crews at the Strategic Air Command post near Omaha, Nebraska. But at 2:26 A.M. that routine was suddenly shattered when computer screens showed that two submarine-launched ballistic missiles were heading toward the United States. Soon more missiles appeared on the screens, and an inquiry to other command posts around the country revealed that their computers showed incoming missiles as well. All signs indicated that a nuclear attack was being launched against the United States.

Red warning lights flashed and alarms sounded in the command center. Flight crews ran to their nuclear-armed B-52 bombers and started the powerful engines in preparation for a quick takeoff. In silos hidden across several western states, Minuteman missiles were prepared for launch. As tense seconds ticked away, the pilots waited for their orders to take off. But the orders never came. A check of distant warning radars showed no sign of missiles heading for the United States. The command post officers soon decided that the computer system had malfunctioned and ended the alert at 2:29:12 A.M. The United States had been poised for nuclear war for three minutes and twelve seconds. The computer problem was eventually traced to a faulty forty-six-cent chip.

Newspapers would later publish the story of the malfunctioning computer with such sensational headlines as "Nuclear War Was Only One Moment Away."[48] In reality, of course, it was not. A Senate investigation of the incident concluded that "In no way can it be said that the United States was close to unleashing nuclear war. . . . In a real sense the total system worked properly in that even though the mechanical electronic part produced erroneous information, the human part correctly evaluated it and prevented any irrevocable action."[49]

The faulty computer chip was just one small part of the vast and complex system developed to warn the United States of an enemy attack. It was a system that began with a newly discovered use for radio, which would eventually be called radar.

Seeing with Radio Waves

Early in the twentieth century, inventors were experimenting with a new medium of communication called radio. During these experiments it was discovered that when radio waves encountered a metal object, they were reflected by that object. Further tests showed that, with a sensitive radio receiver, these reflections could be detected and interpreted. British scientists found that radio waves were also reflected by objects in the atmosphere. They used radio to help predict the weather by bouncing waves off thunderstorms and displaying the results on a screen. Before long, the military potential of this new invention became obvious, and in 1935 radio waves were first used to detect an aircraft in flight.

This system, first named radar (for *ra*dio *d*etection *a*nd *r*anging) by the U.S. Navy, became an important weapon in World War II. After the war, scientists began developing peacetime uses for radar. But when the Soviet Union detonated its first atomic bomb in 1949, the United States began looking for ways to detect a nuclear attack. It was decided to deploy radar where it would give the earliest warning of a Soviet attack: the frozen wilderness at the top of the world.

The DEW Line

As possessor of the atomic bomb and long-range airplanes to deliver it, the Soviet Union in the early 1950s posed a distinct threat to the U.S. mainland. If the Soviets were to attack the United States, the most likely course for their bombers would be the shortest route, over the Arctic region and Canada. On February 15, 1954, President Dwight D. Eisenhower authorized the construction of America's Cold War first line of defense against Soviet bombers. Called the Distant Early Warning (DEW) Line, it was a string of radar stations that extended three thousand miles roughly following the Arctic Circle from Alaska across northern Canada to Greenland.

Flapping in the arctic wind, the American flag flies over a radar station along the Distant Early Warning Line.

olate Arctic by aircraft, ships, barges, and tracked vehicles known as "cats." Construction workers had to work bundled in layer upon layer of clothing. "If we didn't have these layers of mitts," said one worker, "that steel would stick to your hands and burn the flesh right off of you. But working with these mitts is almost like eating grapes with boxing gloves."[50]

The DEW Line radars were designed to detect and identify aircraft flying more than two hundred miles from the station at altitudes of up to 150,000 feet. When an aircraft entered the field of the radar transmitter, an alarm sounded to alert the operator that a target had been spotted. The stations were manned twenty-four hours a day by U.S. and Canadian personnel. Any intrusion would be reported to the North American Air Defense Command (NORAD) headquartered in Colorado Springs, Colorado. Established in 1957 soon after the DEW Line became operational, NORAD's mission was to coordinate U.S. and Canadian defense forces. If NORAD determined that the target was hostile, U.S. jet fighters would be scrambled to intercept the attacking aircraft, and bombers would be readied for a retaliatory strike against the Soviet Union.

Fifty-seven radar stations were built between 1955 and 1957. It was a staggering construction job performed under some of the harshest weather conditions on Earth. Almost half a million tons of material had to be transported to the des-

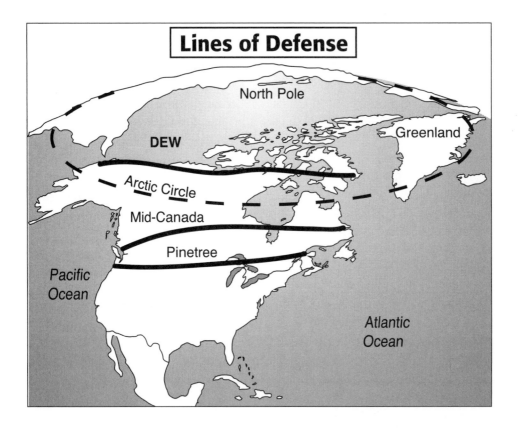

Lines of Defense

North Pole

DEW

Greenland

Arctic Circle

Mid-Canada

Pinetree

Pacific
Ocean

Atlantic
Ocean

In addition to the DEW Line, two other lines of radar stations were constructed in the 1950s: the Pine Tree Line, which stretched along the U.S.-Canadian border, and the Mid-Canada Line, running through central Canada between the other two lines. Radar-equipped aircraft, U.S. Navy picket ships in the northern Pacific Ocean, and radar towers in the Atlantic Ocean off the New England coast supplemented the land-based radar stations. The three lines of defense provided an element critical to protecting North America against a nuclear attack: time. Even the fastest Soviet bombers would take hours to reach the United States. "That DEW Line gives us time," commented an air force officer, "and time is what we need. We get from four to six hours of warning, at present jet speeds, from the second a blip hits their radar."[51] But the time available to respond to an attack would soon be drastically shortened.

BMEWS

By the early 1960s the arms race accelerated and intercontinental ballistic missiles had become the major weapon of the superpowers. Approaching North

America at speeds of two thousand miles per hour or more, Soviet nuclear missile warheads could zoom past existing radar lines and strike targets in North America almost before they were detected. To counter this new threat, the Ballistic Missile Early Warning System (BMEWS) was established. BMEWS is a series of three huge radar stations located in Alaska, Greenland, and Great Britain that became operational between 1960 and 1964. Utilizing giant radar antennas the size of football fields standing on edge,

BMEWS can detect an incoming missile more than three thousand miles away. Using BMEWS, NORAD would have about fifteen to thirty minutes' notice of incoming missiles—not a lot of time, but better than no time at all. Throughout the Cold War years, BMEWS was upgraded to keep pace with advancing technologies of nuclear weapons and delivery vehicles.

The Ballistic Missile Early Warning System was the first operational missile detection system, a military project

Ballistic Missile Early Warning System

U.S.S.R.

Moscow•

Japan

Fylingsdale, England

Spain

Thule, Greenland

• Clear, Alaska

Atlantic Ocean

Pacific Ocean

★ NORAD Colorado Springs, CO

Life on the BMEWS Line

Thule sits near the top of the world on the Danish island of Greenland. It was one of three sites chosen for the Ballistic Missile Early Warning System, a network of radar installations built to detect hostile intercontinental ballistic missiles that may approach North America over the North Pole. The challenging life at the Thule (pronounced TOOL-ee) BMEWS station was described by electronics technician Gene P. McManus in his essay "BMEWS—510 Full Days" (at www.bwcinet.com). The 510 days refers to a typical tour of duty at Thule.

If one were to describe Thule in a single word, it would be "harsh." What vegetation exists is small and low to the ground. The relative humidity is very low, staying at 10 percent or less with only rare exception. Most of the snow which fell on the base was not a result of local precipitation, but rather was blown off the ice cap which had hundreds of thousands of square miles of year-round snow. Winter temperatures would hover in the minus 30F range for weeks at a time; summer warmed up to about 55F. With 24-hour daylight, summer, though short, was really quite pleasant.

During the Thule summer, we did a lot of exploring around the base, radar site, and ice cap, hiking the hills between work shifts. There was some wildlife: arctic foxes and hares were regularly seen. Winter storms could become violent. A "Phase 3" storm, the most severe, would pack winds in excess of 100 miles per hour. All the buildings and exposed facilities had to be hardened to withstand these winds. I witnessed one Phase 3 storm over the Christmas, 1961, holidays which saw the anemometers at the BMEWS site "pegged" at 165 miles per hour. During this storm, the temperature rose from minus 35F to above plus 30F in less than eight hours. One of the anemometers blew away during the storm. . . .

Many of the simple things we took for granted at home were difficult at Thule. We couldn't be shipped whole milk, for example. Instead, dried milk products were reconstituted in a relatively large processing plant to "make" milk and dairy products on site. At first the milk looked and tasted weak, but we soon became accustomed to it. Ice cream was also made on site with the reconstituted milk. Unlike the milk, though, I never got used to the ice cream which had a consistency somewhere between wet sand and cold Cream of Wheat, was almost always too sweet, and whose flavor was rarely identifiable.

designed to guard the North American continent against a Soviet nuclear offensive. But how could ordinary citizens prepare themselves for the possibility of a nuclear attack? In the 1950s, the threat of nuclear war, and the anxiety that it produced, was a constant undercurrent of daily life.

The Red Scare

The decade of the 1950s was one of the most economically prosperous decades in U.S. history. Soldiers had returned from World War II eager to resume a normal life in the late 1940s, which meant getting a job and settling down to raise a family. Wartime shortages were over and manufactured goods such as automobiles, re-frigerators, radios, and the new invention called television were in great demand. New houses appeared in sprawling sub-urbs seemingly overnight. But beneath the prosperity lurked a nagging fear that it could all instantly be taken away in the flash of an atomic explosion.

When the United States lost its nuclear monopoly, many Ameri-cans became obsessed with the fear of commu-nism. This "Red Scare" intensified in 1950 when Wisconsin senator Joseph McCarthy said he had proof that Com-munists had infiltrated the U.S. government. Actors, writers, and other creative individu-als were accused of Communist leanings. In 1953 a poll showed that nearly eight out of ten Americans thought that the Soviet Union wanted to take over the world. It is no wonder that in such a tense and antago-nistic atmosphere, peo-ple thought that at any moment Soviet missiles could be launched to-ward the United States.

Turtles and Backyard Shelters

In response to growing fears of a Soviet at-tack, President Harry Truman established the Federal Civil Defense Administration

School children practice a bomb drill during the height of the "Red Scare" in 1955.

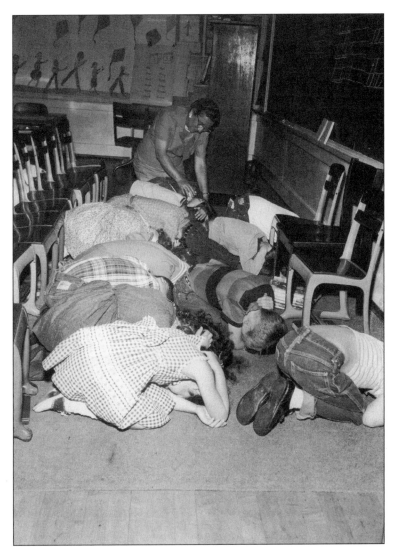

(FCDA) in January 1951. "I cannot tell you," Truman said, "when or where the attack will come, or that it will come at all. I can only remind you that we must be ready when it does come."[52] Created to prepare civilians for surviving a nuclear war, the FCDA produced films, printed material, and television programs designed to educate the American public. Booklets such as *Education for National Survival* were aimed at adults, and comic

books taught children what to do in an air raid. A cartoon character named Bert the Turtle told children to "duck and cover" when a nuclear attack came. Schools held air raid drills like this one described by journalist Todd Gitlin:

> Every so often, out of the blue, a teacher would pause in the middle of class and call out, "Take cover!" We knew, then, to scramble under our

Saving the Government

During the late 1950s and early 1960s, many Americans built fallout shelters to protect their families in case of a nuclear war. Whether these crude constructions would have actually saved anyone from nuclear annihilation is questionable. Meanwhile, U.S. officials were making elaborate secret plans for saving the heads of our government should Soviet missiles rain down on North America.

In one of these plans, named Outpost Mission, an elite team of helicopter pilots would swoop down onto the White House lawn and carry the president, his family, and other administration officials to safety in the event of an expected nuclear assault. The Outpost Mission team was also prepared to rescue the president in case a nuclear attack had already occurred. Dressed in protective suits and carrying digging tools, the team would extract the president from the bunker under the White House and whisk him away to safety. Heavy equipment was also on standby in case the debris of a destroyed White House was too massive for hand tools and cutting torches.

Once rescued, where would the government officials go? Several sites in the eastern United States were prepared to receive the gov-

ernmental elite. Mount Weather, a bunker located in the mountains of Virginia, was completed in 1958 by the Army Corps of Engineers. Protected by a thirty-four-ton blast door, Mount Weather contains living quarters, office spaces, a hospital, dining and recreation facilities, and a radio and television studio. The president, his cabinet, and the Supreme Court would be relocated to Mount Weather in the event of a nuclear attack.

Hidden under a plush West Virginia resort named the Greenbrier lies a three-story shelter designed to save the entire U.S. Congress. Built at a cost of $10 million, the bunker contains dormitories, an operating room, a television studio, and replicas of the House and Senate chambers so that the work of the government could continue uninterrupted. After its existence was discovered and publicized in 1992 by the *Washington Post*, the bunker was closed.

Would these elaborate evacuation plans have actually worked in a nuclear attack? Fortunately, no one has had to find out. But all was not perfect. During one simulated evacuation, as the government convoy approached the entrance to Mount Weather, it was brought to a screeching halt—by a truckload of pigs.

miniature desks and to stay there, cramped, our heads folded under our arms, until the teacher called out, "All clear!" Sometimes the whole school was taken out into the halls, away from the windows, and instructed to crouch down, heads to the walls, our eyes scrunched closed, until further notice.[53]

The FCDA also promoted the building of shelters to protect citizens from an atomic blast and the resulting radioactive fallout. Many cities created public fallout shelters in subway tunnels and basements of large buildings, stocking them with supplies of water, canned food, medical supplies, and Geiger counters to monitor radiation levels. People who wanted more personal protection dug shelters in their own backyards. These private shelters ranged from a deluxe model (which could cost more than $3,000), complete with a telephone and a Geiger counter, to a simple one-room concrete bunker. Those lacking an underground shelter could turn a basement room into a makeshift refuge. Even the U.S. government had top-secret shelters ready in case of an attack.

By the time powerful hydrogen bombs entered the U.S. and Soviet arsenals, it became obvious that no shelter, however well built, could withstand a thermonuclear blast. The Federal Civil Defense Administration decided that mass evacuation from large cities was the only way to save millions of lives. In 1956 President Dwight Eisenhower signed a bill that would create the Interstate Highway System. The system, which eventually stretched across the length and breadth of the United States, was designed to provide not only good roads for commercial and recreational transportation but also escape routes out of major cities that were most likely to be targeted by Soviet ICBMs.

Whether anyone could really escape a nuclear blast or its deadly cloud of radioactive fallout, no one knew for sure. If a method could be developed to stop Soviet missiles from getting to their targets, none of the dubious civil defense measures would be necessary.

The Missile Killers

In the first years of the nuclear arms race, both the United States and the Soviet Union built only offensive missiles designed to attack the enemy in a nuclear war. But as missile technology advanced, the idea arose that perhaps missiles could be used for defensive purposes as well. In the United States, research and development of an antiballistic missile (ABM) system to destroy enemy ICBMs before they reached their targets began in 1956. To track and destroy a missile with another missile is a daunting technological task, described later by President John F. Kennedy as akin to "shooting a bullet with another bullet."[54]

The first U.S. ABM system, called Nike Zeus, was based on earlier systems

A Nike Zeus missile awaits its test launch. Antiballistic missile systems were designed to shoot down enemy missiles.

designed to shoot down enemy aircraft. The system used radar and a computer to detect and track an incoming warhead and guide the Nike Zeus interceptor missile to its target. In July 1962 the Nike Zeus successfully destroyed a test target, proving that the system worked. But several technical problems, including the system's inability to distinguish actual targets from decoys, made the Nike Zeus impractical to deploy. In 1963 another ABM,

called Nike X, was developed. The new system had improved radars and a faster interceptor missile, allowing it to pinpoint the incoming target with greater accuracy and ignore false radar returns. While testing of the Nike X continued, the Soviet Union was working on its own ABM system.

Soviet ABMs

The Soviets had begun developing their own antimissile systems in the late 1950s. In fact, they developed the world's first ABM system, the RZ-25, which was successfully tested in 1961. Unlike the United States, which had only temporarily deployed one ABM system near Grand Forks, North Dakota, the Soviet Union actually put several ABM systems into operation. In 1962 several of the RZ-25 systems were deployed around Leningrad (now St. Petersburg) and the Estonian city of Tallinn. Two years later an improved ABM system was deployed around Moscow, the Soviet capital. This new system used a missile designated by the West as Galosh, which had capabilities similar to the U.S. Nike Zeus.

It would seem that deploying an antiballistic missile system is a logical way to protect a nation from the strategic ICBMs aimed at its missile sites and population centers. Many people, however, felt that the ABM threatened to make nuclear war even more likely. An important proponent of that position was Robert S. McNamara.

The Problem with ABMs

Robert McNamara served from 1961 to 1968 as the U.S. secretary of defense under President Kennedy and his successor, Lyndon Johnson. A graduate of Harvard Business School, McNamara served in the Army Air Force during World War II and worked for Ford Motor Company before turning to public service. It was McNamara who, during his term as secretary of defense, originated the concept of "assured destruction," later known as "mutual assured destruction," or MAD. According to MAD, each superpower now had the ability to destroy the other, so neither would be foolish enough to start a war that it could not win. It was a delicate balance of terror that could be upset by a "destabilizing" force. The ABM, McNamara felt, was one such force.

If one country deploys an ABM system that can protect its population from an enemy's missiles, that country might be tempted to start a nuclear war because its casualties would be limited. McNamara was opposed to the deployment of ABM systems. One of his biographers summarizes McNamara's view of the ABM problem: "Both sides must refrain from a race in damage-limiting systems, such as ABMs, in order to remain terrified of the mortal blow to their societies that the other side's offense could inflict."[55] Since the Soviet Union already had some ABM systems in place, Congress thought that it was time the United States deployed its own ABMs. In 1966 Congress appropriated $168 million to put the Nike X ABM system into production, but President Johnson, agreeing with McNamara, refused to spend the funds.

In early 1967 the Joint Chiefs of Staff (the heads of the U.S. military services) recommended the deployment of an ABM system. McNamara again objected, telling President Johnson, "The chiefs' recommendation is wrong; it's absolutely wrong. The proper response to a Soviet ABM system is not the deployment of an admittedly 'leaky' U.S. defense. The proper response is action which will ensure that we maintain our deterrent capability in the face of the Soviet defense."[56] Johnson and McNamara saw, however, that something had to be done in response to Soviet ABMs, so a compromise was reached. The United States would allocate a small sum for ABMs in the defense budget, but the money would not be spent until an agreement to limit further ABM deployment by both sides could be negotiated.

At first, the Soviets refused even to discuss an ABM treaty. But in 1967 a small step of progress was taken in a rather unlikely place: the small town of Glassboro, New Jersey.

Soviet Premier Aleksei Kosygin and President Lyndon Johnson speak before the Glassboro Summit.

The Glassboro Summit

In June 1967 Soviet premier Aleksei Kosygin was in New York to attend a session of the United Nations when a summit meeting was arranged for him to discuss nuclear arms, including the ABM, with President Johnson. Kosygin would not travel to Washington, however, so the summit took place roughly halfway between New York and Washington on the campus of Glassboro State College (now Rowan University) in Glassboro, New Jersey.

On June 23, the first day of the summit meeting, Secretary of Defense McNamara explained to the Soviet premier the U.S. position on the dangers of ABM systems and the resulting escalation of the arms race. McNamara told Kosygin, "You must understand that the proper U.S. response to your Soviet ABM system is an expansion of our offensive force. . . . Deployment of a Soviet ABM system will lead to an escalation of the arms race. That's not good for either one of us."[57] Kosygin defended his ABM systems, angrily responding, "Defense is moral; offense is immoral!"[58]

Kosygin had stood firm on his ABMs, and the United States needed to respond. Meanwhile, China, which became a Communist nation in 1949, had become a nuclear power as well. It had recently detonated its own hydrogen bomb and was expected to have long-range missile capability within a few years. So President Johnson decided to move forward with the "light deployment" of a U.S. ABM sys-

tem called Sentinel, which was estimated to cost $5 billion. In announcing the decision, McNamara said that deployment of the Sentinel system "in no way indicates that we feel an agreement with the Soviet Union on the limitation of strategic nuclear offensive and defensive forces is in any way less urgent or desirable."[59]

Although no major agreement came out of the Glassboro summit, the meeting was nevertheless a small step forward in arms limitation. It may have led the Soviets, for the first time, to begin taking a serious look at the arms race and the dire consequences that could result from further escalation.

SALT

In early 1968 the Soviet Union indicated that it was willing to begin pursuing arms control talks with the United States. This concession came, in part, from the fact that the cost of building a nuclear arsenal had put a severe strain on the already shaky Soviet economy. In a nation where agriculture and industry lagged seriously behind other modern countries, the Soviet Union could ill afford another round of military escalation. Soviet foreign minister Andrei Gromyko announced that his country was willing to discuss "mutual limitation and subsequent reduction of strategic means of delivery of nuclear weapons, both offensive and defensive, including antiballistic missiles."[60] The negotiations, called Strategic Arms Limitation Talks, or SALT, were scheduled to

Members of SALT I meet in Helsinki, Finland, to discuss limiting the number of antiballistic missiles.

begin in September 1968. But in response to growing unrest and the establishment of some democratic reforms in Communist Czechoslovakia, Soviet troops invaded that country in August, putting the talks on hold for more than a year.

Teams of U.S. and Soviet negotiators met for the first round of talks, called SALT I, on November 7, 1969, in Helsinki, Finland. Seven subsequent meetings were held over a period of two and a half years, alternating between Helsinki and Vienna, Austria. Discussions ranged from identifying the missiles that were to be included in the "strategic forces" sub-

ject to limitation to the relationship of offensive weapons systems to ABMs. One point that became clear early on was that the Soviets were extremely interested in stopping the deployment of a U.S. ABM system. Richard Nixon, who had succeeded Lyndon Johnson as president, told U.S. negotiators that they should make no agreement on ABMs that did not include the reduction of offensive missiles as well.

As a result of both the formal talks and secret "back channel" negotiations, the first Strategic Arms Limitation Talks produced the SALT I Treaty, which was signed on May 26, 1972. The treaty was made up of two agreements. The first agreement, the Antiballistic Missile Treaty, limited the number of ABM sites the United States and the Soviet Union could have to only two, one to protect the nation's capital and the other to defend an ICBM site (this was later reduced to only one site per nation). In addition, no more than one hundred missiles were allowed at each site. The second agreement, called the Interim Agreement on the Limitation of Strategic Offensive Arms, limited the number of strategic missile launchers (and, in effect, missiles) that each nation could have over the next five years. The United States was limited to the missiles already in its arsenal: 1,054 ICBMs and 710 SLBMs. The Soviet Union's arsenal was capped at 1,618 ICBMs and 950 SLBMs. Although this allowed the Soviet Union a greater number of missiles, U.S. negotiators agreed to the numbers because of the inherent technical superiority of U.S. weapons. As with the Partial Test Ban Treaty, national means of verification would be used to ensure that neither superpower tried to cheat on the agreements.

Though the SALT I Treaty, for the most part, simply froze the current levels of strategic weapons, it was, in political terms, a real start to arms control. It cre-ated a thaw in the Cold War and gave the Soviet Union the political recognition it desired: to be seen as a legitimate strategic equal to the United States in the eyes of the world. For the United States, and certainly for the Soviet Union as well, there were financial benefits to SALT I. As Gerard Smith, the chief U.S. negotiator at SALT, wrote, "The negotiations cost the taxpayers about $6 million. Net SALT savings in the 1973 defense budget alone were about $800 million. Estimated longer-term savings from not having a four-site ABM program were $11 to $13 billion."[61]

Congressman Gerald Ford (who would later become president upon Nixon's resignation) said, "What it all comes down to is this. We did not give anything away, and we slowed the Soviet momentum in the nuclear arms race."[62] SALT I would be followed by another round of arms limitation talks. But the next negotiations would not be so successful.

SALT II

Under the terms of SALT I, the superpowers pledged to continue negotiations aimed at further limiting strategic arms. The new discussions, called SALT II, began in November 1972, just six months after SALT I was signed. The goal of U.S. negotiators was to replace SALT I's interim agreement on strategic arms, which was effective for only five years, with a long-term pact. They wanted to establish equal numbers of strategic weapons for the United States and the Soviet Union and then begin the process of reducing these numbers. Two years of difficult negotiations followed.

In November 1974 President Gerald Ford met with Soviet general secretary Leonid Brezhnev in the Soviet city of Vladivostok to set up a framework for a SALT II agreement. The basic framework allowed each side to have 2,400 strategic nuclear launchers and a limit of 1,320 multiple independently targeted reentry vehicle systems. Construction of new land-based missile launchers was banned, and the deployment of new types of strategic weapons was limited. This new agreement, if approved by both superpowers, would remain in effect until 1985.

Negotiations continued toward the goal of producing an agreement based on the Vladivostok framework. The United States presented several proposals for a treaty, but each was rejected by the Soviets as not being in line with the Vladivostok accord. Finally, an agreement acceptable to both sides was reached; the SALT II Treaty was signed on June 18, 1979, by President Jimmy Carter and Soviet general secretary Brezhnev. Four days later, Carter sent the agreement to the Senate for ratification.

But the SALT II Treaty would not be approved. In December 1979 Soviet troops invaded Afghanistan, a nation located across the Soviet Union's southern

Dealing with the Russians

Negotiating arms treaties with the Soviet Union during the Strategic Arms Limitation Talks was difficult. As quoted in the book *Inside the Cold War: An Oral History* by John Sharnik, U.S. negotiator Paul Warnke explains the reticence of his Soviet counterparts across the negotiating table.

> One of the real problems we've had with the Soviet Union is their preoccupation with secrecy. And it's a secrecy that predates the Bolshevik Revolution [when Russia became a Communist nation in 1917]. When you read accounts of people trying to deal with the czars back in the seventeenth, eighteenth, nineteenth centuries, you find that this preoccupation with secrecy is basically a Russian trait.
>
> Now, as a consequence, we had great difficulty getting the Soviet Union to accept

> something that we thought was quite routine, and that was the exchange of a data base. We wanted a listing by both sides of all relevant categories of strategic weapons. The Soviet Union fought that for years.
>
> And I can remember, finally, when the Soviet side accepted that. It took a trip back to the Soviet Union by Minister [Vladimir] Semenov. And he finally came in to Ralph Earl, who was the deputy head of the delegation, and me and said, "I am now authorized to exchange the data base." And then he said, "you realize that you've just repealed about four hundred years of Russian history." And then he further said, "And maybe that's not a bad idea."

Soviet general secretary Leonid Brezhnev kisses U.S. president Jimmy Carter. The SALT II Treaty was solidified two days later.

border. In response to this invasion, Carter withdrew the treaty from Senate consideration. Under international law, both nations were still bound to abide by the terms of the treaty, unless they intentionally withdrew from it. To their credit, both Carter and Brezhnev agreed to do nothing to violate the terms of the unratified treaty. So the provisions of SALT II remained, even though the treaty was officially in limbo. However, relations between the United States and the Soviet Union, which had seemed to be warming after SALT I, once again cooled. Although the abject fear of a nuclear holocaust prevalent in the 1950s and 1960s had diminished in the American mind, the Cold War would live on—on Earth and in space.

Chapter 6

Arming Space, Disarming Earth

cience fiction had long been a popular form of entertainment when the Soviet satellite *Sputnik* suddenly boosted space exploration from science fiction to scientific fact. America's ultimate triumph in space came on July 20, 1969, when astronaut Neil Armstrong's words— "That's one small step for man, one giant leap for mankind"—were beamed to Earth as he became the first human to set foot on the moon. It was a milestone in human history as well as the culmination of a decade of intensive research and development by the National Aeronautics and Space Administration. But what began as the peaceful exploration of space soon gave way to the realities of politics here on Earth. For in the midst of the Cold War, man began looking for a way to send his weapons of war into this new and uncharted realm.

Space Bombs and ASATs

When *Sputnik* orbited the earth in 1957, Americans feared that the Soviets might soon launch other satellites carrying bombs that could be dropped without warning on the United States. Although those fears seemed irrational at the time, a few years later the Soviet Union was developing just such a weapon. In 1966, after several years of research, the Soviets began testing a space-based nuclear weapons platform called the Fractional Orbiting Bombardment System, or FOBS. With FOBS, a Soviet missile would place a nuclear warhead into a low orbit about one hundred miles above the earth. But before the warhead made one complete revolution of the earth (hence the name "fractional" because it would travel only a fraction of an orbit), retro-rockets would be fired, sending the warhead back through the atmosphere and to its target. The advantage of an orbiting bombardment system is that it can attack the United States from any direction, especially over the South Pole, to which northern-facing early warning radars are blind. In effect, the warhead would act like a very-long-range ICBM that could bypass the BMEWS warning radars by sneaking in undetected from the south. After a series of test flights, FOBS was put into service in November 1968.

The United States never developed an orbiting bombardment system like FOBS. But it had already begun looking for ways to counter the possible Soviet military use of satellites. The first anti-satellite (ASAT) program was developed by the United States under the name Project SAINT. Begun around 1959, Project SAINT (which stood for SAtellite INTerceptor) consisted of a satellite launched into space so that its orbit matched that of a suspicious Soviet satellite. If, after inspecting the target with television cameras, the SAINT satellite determined it to be an offensive weapon, the interceptor would destroy it by blowing it up, ramming it, or some other means. It was a bold concept, but political and financial setbacks caused the cancellation of Project SAINT in 1962.

U.S. planners experimented with two nuclear antisatellite systems. One system, called Program 505 or Operation Mudflap, used a modified Nike Zeus ABM to launch a nuclear warhead on an interception trajectory toward an enemy satellite. The first successful test intercept of this system was made in May 1963. But the Nike Zeus's limited altitude capability resulted in its replacement with another program. Program 427 utilized a Thor in-termediate range ballistic missile to destroy satellites at altitudes of more than four hundred miles. This system was deployed in 1964 and remained operational until 1975. Other ASAT systems proposed launching satellite-killing missiles from jet fighters or bombers.

The Soviet Union developed its own ASATs under the umbrella of the Cosmos satellite program. In 1972, U.S. intelligence announced that the Soviets had conducted at least eighteen ASAT tests since 1967, successfully destroying several of their own satellites in the tests. The Soviet system was apparently similar to the abandoned U.S. SAINT program, and an official U.S. report warned that space could become an arena for international conflict. But then, to the confusion of U.S. officials, the Soviets stopped testing their ASATs, only to resume in 1976.

In 1980 Ronald Reagan was elected president, succeeding Jimmy Carter. As his administration began, relations between the United States and the Soviet Union were at their worst point in years. Détente, the period of thawed relations that characterized the 1970s, was over. The continued Soviet presence in Afghanistan and the downing of a Korean airliner by a Soviet jet fighter kept tensions between the superpowers high. Reagan appeared to have no interest in negotiating with a nation that he would later characterize as the "evil empire." During Reagan's administration, the Soviet

Star Wars

In the summer of 1979, four months before he announced his candidacy for president, Ronald Reagan visited the headquarters of the North American Aerospace Defense Command located deep under Cheyenne Mountain in Colorado. There, he saw firsthand how the military would track Soviet missiles launched toward the United States and coordinate a retaliatory strike. The command center's huge electronic maps, display screens, and computers impressed Reagan, but the future president was disturbed by something he did not see. Despite all the sophisticated tracking systems and dedicated personnel, there was no way to stop a Soviet attack once the missiles were air-

A mechanic tightens a screw on a Thor rocket, the United States' intermediate range ballistic missile satellite-killing system.

Union would begin its decline toward dissolution. But during his first term, Reagan proposed one of the most controversial programs of the nuclear arms race—a new outer space missile defense system.

borne. "We have spent all that money," one writer reports Reagan as saying, "and have all that equipment, and there is nothing we can do to prevent a nuclear missile from hitting us. . . . We should have some way of defending ourselves against nuclear missiles."[63] When he became president, Reagan was determined to find a way.

After taking office, Reagan set up a group to study the feasibility of a new ballistic missile defense (BMD) system. The group met in secret, keeping even high-ranking administration officials, including the secretaries of defense and state, in the dark. Secretary of State George Schultz described it as "a very personal project. It was very much driven by Ronald Reagan."[64] Reagan did have at least one well-known, if controversial, adviser. Physicist Edward Teller, the "father of the hydrogen bomb," told Reagan he had an idea for a new device—an X-ray laser—that showed promise for a missile defense system. Powered by a nuclear explosion, Teller's laser, at least in theory, could destroy thousands of Soviet warheads at once, making it a weapon of devastating power and extreme value. It is, however, unclear just how much influence Teller had on the president's thinking.

On the evening of March 23, 1983, President Reagan addressed the nation on network television. The speech was about Reagan's concerns for national security and included the first public mention of his proposed new missile defense initiative:

Taking the oath of office, President Ronald Reagan vowed to begin an outer space missile defense system.

Let me share with you a vision of the future which offers hope. It is that we embark on a program to counter the awesome Soviet missile threat with measures that are defensive. . . . Up until now we have increasingly based our strategy of deterrence upon the threat of retaliation. But what if free people could live secure in the knowledge that their security did not rest upon the threat of instant U.S. retaliation to deter a Soviet attack; that we could intercept and destroy strategic ballistic missiles before they reached our own soil or that of our allies? . . . I call upon the scientific community

who gave us nuclear weapons to turn their great talents to the cause of mankind and world peace; to give us the means of rendering these nuclear weapons impotent and obsolete.[65]

Negative reaction to Reagan's speech was almost immediate. While it sounded like a good idea to some, many people were not even sure what Reagan had been talking about. Could he be calling for a revival of the old ABM systems, updated with the latest exotic technology? Newspapers generally treated the proposal as either a scandal, a political ploy, or a half-baked scheme based more on

The Outer Space Treaty

In 1967, as the space race between the United States and the Soviet Union was in full swing, people began thinking seriously about the dangers posed by orbiting nuclear weapons. The result was the Outer Space Treaty, which was designed to guarantee the peaceful use of outer space. The full text of the treaty, from which the following excerpt was taken, can be found on the U.S. State Department's website (www.state.gov):

Article IV

States Parties to the Treaty undertake not to place in orbit around the Earth any objects carrying nuclear weapons or any other kinds of weapons of mass destruction, install such weapons on celestial bodies, or station such weapons in outer space in any other manner.

The Moon and other celestial bodies shall be used by all States Parties to the Treaty ex-

clusively for peaceful purposes. The establishment of military bases, installations and fortifications, the testing of any type of weapons and the conduct of military maneuvers on celestial bodies shall be forbidden. The use of military personnel for scientific research or for any other peaceful purposes shall not be prohibited. The use of any equipment or facility necessary for peaceful exploration of the Moon and other celestial bodies shall also not be prohibited.

Would President Reagan's Star Wars program have violated the Outer Space Treaty? While the treaty prohibits "weapons of mass destruction," this phrase is usually understood to mean nuclear weapons. Since Star Wars would have used lasers and particle beam weapons, it would probably not have been prohibited. But Reagan's dream was never put into practice, so the question of its legality is left to theoretical speculation.

science fiction than on scientific fact. In fact, soon the media had dubbed the president's initiative "Star Wars" after the popular science fiction movie.

Ronald Reagan's dream of an impenetrable defensive shield against nuclear weapons would become officially known as the Strategic Defense Initiative (SDI). But the road ahead for SDI was rough and, as it turned out, an endlessly meandering path toward oblivion.

Problems with SDI

From the beginning, Star Wars technology, in the form of Edward Teller's X-ray laser, experienced problems. Despite Teller's enthusiastic (some said overly optimistic) view that his laser could be put into operation quickly, experts agreed that the technology was so complex and untried that it would not be ready for some twenty years and then only in a limited capacity. Tests of the system gave inconclusive results. An additional problem was the fact that the X-ray laser needed a nuclear explosion to create the X rays that would destroy enemy warheads. In his speech, Reagan had said he wanted to make nuclear arms "impotent and obsolete." Yet here was a system that depended on the very technology that Reagan wanted to eliminate.

With the X-ray laser looking more and more unworkable, another system was proposed. Called Brilliant Pebbles, this system would rely on thousands of small orbiting interceptors (the "pebbles") that could seek out and destroy enemy warheads on command. A political advantage of Brilliant Pebbles was that, unlike the X-ray laser, it involved no nuclear devices; as a so-called kinetic energy weapon, each interceptor would simply use its speed and mass to knock out its target. With his X-ray laser out of favor, Edward Teller began promoting Brilliant Pebbles.

As Star Wars research continued throughout the 1980s, both the United States and the Soviet Union began to realize that they should talk once more about limiting nuclear arms. The Soviets, unable to match the United States in the technology needed for a Star Wars–type defensive system, did not want to see the United States pull ahead in space-based systems. For his part, President Reagan was changing his ideas of the "evil empire." "I emphasize once again," Reagan said in a radio broadcast, "America's desire for genuine cooperation between our two countries. Together we can make the world a better, more peaceful place."[66] However, he remained committed to his dream of a missile shield over America. That commitment would play an important role in the negotiating process.

A New START

The Strategic Arms Limitation Talks (SALT I and II) dealt with limiting the numbers of nuclear weapons possessed by the United States and the Soviet Union. The two superpowers were holding to the provisions of the SALT II agreement, even though it had not been ratified. In 1981 Reagan proposed that the two nations begin a new round of talks aimed at reducing the number of strategic nuclear weapons, not just freezing them at current levels. To distinguish them from the previous SALT negotiations, these new negotiations would be called Strategic Arms Reduction Talks, or START.

The first START session between U.S. and Soviet negotiators was held on June 29, 1982. For the next several years, the talks centered on proposals and counter proposals by both sides for various levels of reduction in ICBM forces. It was dur-

ing this period that Reagan made his televised announcement of the Star Wars project. This presented a new problem for the U.S. negotiators, because the Soviets refused to agree to strategic arms reductions unless the United States abandoned, or at least limited, its plans for Star Wars.

In March 1985 Mikhail Gorbachev became general secretary of the Soviet Communist Party and leader of the Soviet

Mikhail Gorbachev, general secretary of the Soviet Communist Party instituted major social and economic reforms in the Soviet Union.

Union. He began a program of major economic and social reforms in the Soviet Union that would come to be known as glasnost (openness) and perestroika (restructuring). In the interest of improving U.S.-Soviet relations, Reagan wrote to the new Soviet leader, inviting him to visit Washington. Gorbachev was reluctant to come to the U.S. capital, so a summit meeting was arranged for that November in Geneva, Switzerland. Reagan's mission was "to engage the new Soviet leader in what I hope will be a dialog for peace that endures beyond my presidency."[67]

During the two-day summit held at a lakeside villa, the two leaders talked about freeing the world from the long-held policy of mutual assured destruction. Reagan told Gorbachev, "I simply cannot condone the notion of keeping peace by threatening to blow each other away. We must be able to find a better way."[68] For Reagan, that way was, of course, the Strategic Defense Initiative. When he presented Gorbachev a proposal for reducing offensive nuclear arms—a proposal that included further research on SDI—the Soviet leader balked. After Reagan repeated that SDI must continue, Gorbachev ended the discussion with a curt, "Then we just disagree."[69] Reagan offered to share information on SDI research with the Soviet Union, but the gesture elicited no enthusiasm from Gorbachev.

The Geneva summit ended with no new arms agreements, although both sides promised to conduct further talks aimed at reducing the nuclear arsenal of both nations by 50 percent. However, the two leaders had forged the beginning of a new, more cordial relationship between the superpowers, and Reagan observed that he had "finally met a Soviet leader I could talk to."[70]

Stalemate—or Breakthrough— in Iceland

Reagan and Gorbachev met for another summit in October 1986. This time the location was Reykjavik, the capital of Iceland. Hopes for a new agreement soared during the weekend summit at Hofdi House, a former British ambassador's villa overlooking the Atlantic Ocean. This time at the negotiating table, Reagan and Gorbachev discussed the possibility of eliminating intermediate range nuclear missiles in Europe and eventually dismantling all strategic missiles. Reagan again offered to share U.S. SDI research and agreed not to deploy such a system for ten years. Surprisingly, Gorbachev brought numerous concessions to the bargaining table. He agreed to a reduction in Soviet conventional (non-nuclear) forces in Europe and resolved to comply with adequate verification procedures to ensure that terms were being met. Spirits were high among the American delegates; they could hardly believe the negotiations were going so well.

Toward the end of the summit, however, Gorbachev dropped a bombshell. As

Learning from the Cold War

As the Cold War entered its fourth decade, many people began looking back at what had been accomplished and at what was yet to be done to eliminate the threat of nuclear weapons from the world. Dean Rusk, secretary of state under Presidents Kennedy and Johnson from 1961 to 1969, related some of his thoughts on the Cold War to John Sharnik in his book *Inside the Cold War: An Oral History.*

> In 1985 we put behind us forty years since a nuclear weapon had been fired in anger, despite several serious and even dangerous crises. We've learned during those forty years that the fingers on the nuclear triggers are not itchy, just waiting for a pretext to fire. We've learned that Soviet leaders have no more interest in destroying Mother Russia than our leaders have in destroying our beloved America.

> Now, that's not a guarantee for the future. We and the Soviets should not play games of chicken with each other to see how far one can go without crossing that lethal line. And we have to watch the level of rhetoric between our two countries, because if that rhetoric becomes too virulent over too long a period of time, there's always that one side or the other will begin to believe its own rhetoric, and then we could have problems.

> Throughout human history, it's been possible for the human race to pick itself up out of the death and destruction of war and start over again. We shan't have that chance after World War III—there won't be enough left. So, at long last, the human race has reached the point where it must prevent that war before it occurs.

the agreements were being finalized, Gorbachev said, "This all depends, of course, on you giving up SDI."[71] Suddenly the reasons for Gorbachev's concessions became clear: He was desperate to undermine SDI. Angered by the Soviet inflexibility on Star Wars, Reagan abruptly ended the meeting. He recalled that day in his diary: "He [Gorbachev] wanted language that would have killed SDI. The price was high but I wouldn't sell and that's how the day ended. All our people thought I'd done exactly right. I'd pledged I wouldn't give away SDI and I didn't, but that meant no deal on any of the arms reductions. He tried to act jovial but I was mad and showed it."[72]

As another summit that ended without an agreement, Reykjavik was characterized by some as a failure. Others saw it differently, as Jack Matlock, special assistant to the president, recalls:

In a sense, the failure at Reykjavik gave the Soviets another push to start to open up their society and to deal with human rights issues. . . . So Reykjavik was the hinge summit; it was a breakthrough—probably the most important summit we had. What was decided there—with one or two exceptions of detail—eventually became the treaties. So to look at it as a failure is to look at it in a very superficial way.[73]

Another government official told the president, "You've really come through; you just won the cold war."[74] Although the Cold War was still a few years from being won, the Soviet Union under Mikhail Gorbachev was exhibiting a relaxation of its former hard-line policies. And with the new Soviet demeanor came real progress on slowing down the arms race. Soon, an entire class of nuclear weapons would be erased from the face of the earth.

Reducing the Arsenals

By 1987 the nuclear stockpiles of the two superpowers had grown to immense proportions. The Soviet arsenal numbered a staggering forty-three thousand nuclear warheads of all types. The United States had more than twenty-three thousand warheads deployed on land- and submarine-based missiles and in bombers. This total included warheads on hundreds of nonstrategic (intermediate or short-range) missiles making up the intermediate range nuclear forces (INF). These U.S. missiles—Pershing IIs—were deployed by NATO in Europe to counter the threat of Soviet SS-20 intermediate range missiles. For years, the nations of NATO had wanted to reduce the threat of a nuclear war on European soil. The Soviets also hoped to remove the missiles that were within just a few minutes' flight time from their homeland.

Reagan (left) and Gorbachev converse after unsuccessful disarmament discussions in Iceland.

Able Archer 83

In 1962, during the Kennedy administration, the United States and the Soviet Union came close to nuclear war over Soviet missiles stationed in Cuba. Twenty-one years later, Ronald Reagan was president during another nuclear near-mishap. Unlike the Cuban Missile Crisis, Able Archer remains relatively obscure in the annals of Cold War history. Most people would not even recognize the name. But it brought the world once more to the brink of nuclear war.

In the fall of 1983, tensions between the United States and the Soviet Union were on the rise. On September 1 Soviet fighters shot down a Korean airliner, resulting in the deaths of 269 people. In October the U.S. Army invaded the Caribbean island of Granada to prevent a Communist takeover. Soviet leader Yuri Andropov, although seriously ill, was concerned that the invasion might portend something worse.

Then just one week later, the United States and its allies in NATO began a military exercise code-named Able Archer 83. The massive exercise was designed to practice nuclear launch procedures that would be used in the event of a nuclear attack against the Soviet Union and its Warsaw Pact allies. More than 300,000 civilians and military personnel took part in the exercise, which covered Europe from Scandinavia to the Mediterranean. President Reagan was scheduled to participate but did not do so for fear of making Able Archer appear too provocative.

The Soviet leadership was already wary of Reagan; after all, he had called the Soviet Union an "evil empire." Now, as Soviet intelligence followed the progress of Able Archer, Andropov became alarmed. Could this exercise be a cover for a U.S. first strike against the Soviet Union? Urgent "flash" telegrams were sent, warning Soviet agents in Europe that U.S. troops in Europe were being mobilized. Soviet aircraft armed with nuclear weapons were put on alert and began to prepare for a counterattack.

Fortunately, Able Archer 83 ended without incident. For reasons that can only be guessed at, no one in the Soviet Union pushed the nuclear "button" to start what might very well have been World War III. But Able Archer did affect President Reagan's view of the Soviet Union. He was astonished that Soviet leaders actually feared a U.S. first strike. As he relates in his autobiography, *An American Life*,

> The more experience I had with Soviet leaders . . . the more I began to realize that many Soviet officials feared us not only as adversaries but as potential aggressors who might hurl nuclear weapons at them in a first strike. . . . Well, if that was the case, I was even more anxious to get a top Soviet leader in a room alone and try to convince him we had no designs on the Soviet Union and Russians had nothing to fear from us.

Negotiations with the Soviet Union over the INF missiles had begun late in the Carter administration. At the time there were no Pershing II missiles in Europe, but the decision to deploy them had already been made. So the Soviet position centered on preventing their deployment. When Reagan took over, he championed a "zero option" plan that called for both the United States and the Soviet Union to have no nuclear missiles whatsoever in Europe. The Soviets, who had already deployed their SS-20s, rejected the idea out of hand: Why should they remove their missiles when the United States had nothing but a promise to give up? At this impasse the talks stalled, and in December 1983 the first Pershing IIs became operational in Europe.

At the Reykjavik summit, INF missiles had been a part of the negotiations that abruptly ended because of Gorbachev's objections to Star Wars. But in February 1987, signs were appearing that the Soviet Union was willing to negotiate INF. A Soviet news release said, in part, "The Soviet Union suggests that the problem of medium-range missiles in Europe be singled out from the package of issues, and that a separate agreement on it be concluded, and without delay."[75]

From that point on, negotiators moved swiftly, working out the details of what would become an INF agreement. On December 8, 1987, Reagan and Gorbachev signed the INF Treaty at a summit meeting in Washington. The treaty, which became effective on June 1, 1988, called for the destruction of 846 U.S. intermediate and short-range missiles, including the Pershing IIs. The Soviet Union was required to destroy 1,846 missiles, which included the SS-20s. Also included in the treaty was a detailed system

Gorbachev (left) and Reagan sign the INF Treaty.

of on-site inspections to ensure that the provisions of the agreement were carried out. By May 1991 the last INF missile had been destroyed.

The INF Treaty was a groundbreaking agreement. For the first time in the history of the nuclear arms race, the superpowers had agreed to eliminate, not just reduce, the number of nuclear weapons in their arsenals. The world had been made a little bit safer. But the most awesome and destructive nuclear weapons, the intercontinental ballistic missiles, still remained in their silos and submarines and aircraft bomb bays. Could a START agreement begin to eliminate those missiles too?

Signing START

Both Reagan and Gorbachev would benefit politically by a signed START agreement, and both seemed ready to get to work on it. In fact, the basic ceilings to which the arsenals would be reduced had been agreed to at the Reykjavik summit. In May 1987 the United States summarized these limits in a draft of a proposed START treaty presented at a negotiating session in Geneva. Two months later the Soviet Union presented its own draft as a counterproposal to the U.S. version. Talks continued over the next several years as negotiators hammered out an agreement in sessions in Geneva, Moscow, and Washington.

President Reagan would not preside over the conclusion of the START negoti-

ations he began in 1982. George Herbert Walker Bush, Reagan's vice president, was elected to the nation's top office in November 1988. On July 31, 1991, Bush and Gorbachev met in Washington to sign the Treaty on the Reduction and Limitation of Strategic Offensive Arms, also known as the START treaty. Both sides would be limited to 1,600 strategic nuclear delivery vehicles (missiles, submarines, and bombers), and the number of nuclear warheads on these vehicles could not exceed 6,000. Of those warheads, 4,900 could be mounted on ballistic missiles deployed in silos or submarines and 1,100 on mobile ICBMs. As a result of these cuts, the number of nuclear warheads would be reduced by 20 to 30 percent.

An Uncertain Future

Five months after the signing of the START treaty, however, the Soviet Union ceased to exist as a nation. On December 25, 1991, Mikhail Gorbachev resigned as president of the Soviet Union. In fact, it was no longer a true union, for several of the republics that made up the Soviet Union had already become independent. On the last day of 1991, with the Soviet Union no more, the Cold War came to an end.

There was, however, still the matter of the Soviet nuclear arsenal and the START treaty. Four states now had possession of the former Soviet Union's nuclear weapons: Russia, Belarus, Ukraine, and Kazakhstan. All four agreed to abide

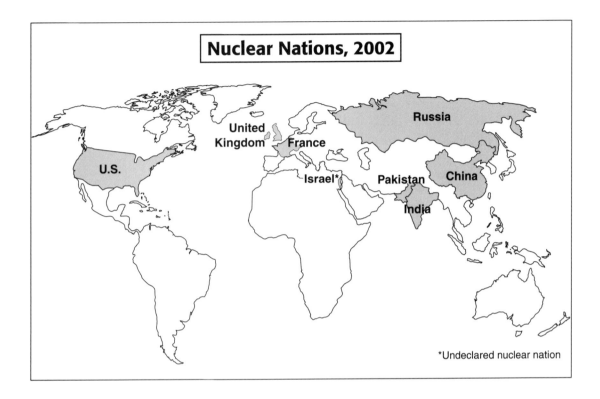

by the START treaty and in 1992 signed the "Lisbon Protocol," with the United States solidifying that agreement. Since then, Belarus, Ukraine, and Kazakhstan have given up their nuclear weapons. In May 2002 President George W. Bush and Russian Federation president Vladimir Putin signed an agreement that mandates cutting their remaining nuclear arsenals by two-thirds by the year 2012. Meanwhile, several smaller countries have developed nuclear weapons. At the beginning of the twenty-first century, eight nations were members of the "nuclear club," and others were seeking nuclear capability.

Fear of terrorist groups obtaining the raw materials for building a nuclear device increased after the September 11, 2001, attacks on New York and Washington, D.C. While the danger of a global nuclear conflict has lessened, the possibility of a limited nuclear conflict still exists and grows more plausible every day. Citing just such a threat, President George W. Bush officially withdrew the United States from the Antiballistic Missile Treaty on June 13, 2002. In force since 1972, the ABM Treaty was designed to prevent destabilization between the United States and the Soviet Union during the Cold War. Bush explained that "we no longer live in the Cold War world for which the ABM Treaty was designed. We now face new threats from terrorists who seek to destroy our civilization by any means available, to rogue states armed with weapons of mass destruction and long range missiles."[76] Two days later near Fairbanks, Alaska, ground was broken for a new U.S. ballistic missile defense system, the kind of system that had been banned by the ABM Treaty for thirty years.

The nuclear arms race of the Cold War years may have ended, but the race for a lasting peace still has a long way to go.

☆ Notes ☆

Introduction:
Weapons Too Terrible to Use

1. H.G. Wells, *The Last War: A World Set Free.* Lincoln: University of Nebraska Press, 2001, p. 60.

Chapter 1: The Ultimate Weapon: The Atomic Bomb

2. Quoted in Richard Rhodes, *The Making of the Atomic Bomb.* New York: Simon and Schuster, 1986, p. 28.
3. Quoted in William Lanouette, with Bela Silard, *Genius in the Shadows: A Biography of Leo Szilard, the Man Behind the Bomb.* New York: Charles Scribner's Sons, 1992, p. 210.
4. Quoted in Leslie R. Groves, *Now It Can Be Told: The Story of the Manhattan Project.* 1962. Reprint: New York: Da Capo Press, 1983, p. 3.
5. Groves, *Now It Can Be Told,* p. 4.
6. Quoted in Rhodes, *The Making of the Atomic Bomb,* p. 424.
7. Quoted in Rhodes, *The Making of the Atomic Bomb,* p. 426.
8. Leona Woods Marshall Libby, *The Uranium People.* New York: Crane, Russak, 1979, p. 86.
9. Quoted in Rhodes, *The Making of the Atomic Bomb,* p. 440.
10. Quoted in Rhodes, *The Making of the Atomic Bomb,* p. 442.
11. Quoted in Rhodes, *The Making of the Atomic Bomb,* p. 442.
12. Groves, *Now It Can Be Told,* p. 69.
13. Groves, *Now It Can Be Told,* p. 61.
14. Quoted in Rhodes, *The Making of the Atomic Bomb,* p. 666.
15. Quoted in Rhodes, *The Making of the Atomic Bomb,* p. 669.
16. Quoted in Rhodes, *The Making of the Atomic Bomb,* p. 672.
17. Groves, *Now It Can Be Told,* p. 298.
18. Quoted in Rhodes, *The Making of the Atomic Bomb,* p. 676.

Chapter 2: The Race Begins: Airborne Weaponry

19. Quoted in David McCullough, *Truman.* New York: Touchstone Books, 1992, p. 377.
20. Quoted in McCullough, *Truman,* p. 378.
21. Quoted in David A. Anderton, *Strategic Air Command: Two-Thirds of the Triad.* New York: Charles Scribner's Sons, 1976, p. 32.

22. Quoted in David Holloway, *Stalin and the Bomb: The Soviet Union and Atomic Energy 1939–1956*. New Haven, CT: Yale University Press, 1944, pp. 205–206.

23. Quoted in Holloway, *Stalin and the Bomb*, p. 216.

24. Quoted in McCullough, *Truman*, p. 749.

25. Quoted in Norman Polmar, *Strategic Weapons: An Introduction*. New York: Crane, Russak, 1975, p. 14.

26. Quoted in Stanley A. Blumberg and Louis G. Panos, *Edward Teller: Giant of the Golden Age of Physics*. New York: Charles Scribner's Sons, 1990, p. 63.

27. Quoted in McCullough, *Truman*, p. 763.

28. Quoted in Richard Rhodes, *Dark Sun: The Making of the Hydrogen Bomb*. New York: Simon and Schuster, 1995, p. 509.

29. Quoted in Blumberg and Panos, *Edward Teller*, p. 141.

30. Quoted in Holloway, *Stalin and the Bomb*, p. 315.

31. Quoted in Holloway, *Stalin and the Bomb*, p. 316.

Chapter 3: The Arms Race on the Ground: Ballistic Missiles

32. Quoted in G. Harry Stine, *ICBM*. New York: Orion Books, 1991, p. 129.

33. Quoted in Dennis Piszkiewicz, *The Nazi Rocketeers: Dreams of Space and Crimes of War*. Westport, CT: Praeger, 1995, p. 224.

34. Quoted in John L. Chapman, *Atlas: The Story of a Missile*. New York: Harper and Brothers, 1960, p. 78.

35. Quoted in Holloway, *Stalin and the Bomb*, p. 247.

36. Quoted in Stine, *ICBM*, p. 157.

37. Quoted in Paul Dickson, *Sputnik: The Shock of the Century*. New York: Walker, 2001, p. 96.

38. Quoted in Dickson, *Sputnik*, p. 150.

39. Quoted in Lawrence Freedman, *The Evolution of Nuclear Strategy*. New York: St. Martin's Press, 1983, p. 244.

40. Quoted in "On 35th Anniversary of JFK Address, World Still Waits for Nuclear Test Ban." Coalition Issue Brief, vol. 2, no. 15, June 10, 1998. www.clw.org.

Chapter 4: The Arms Race at Sea: Completing the Triad

41. Quoted in Norman Polmar and Thomas B. Allen, *Rickover*. New York: Simon and Schuster, 1982, p. 165.

42. Quoted in Chuck Lawliss, *The Submarine Book: An Illustrated History of the Attack Submarine*. Short Hills, NJ: Burford Books, 2000, p. 118.

43. John Piña Craven, *The Silent War: The Cold War Battle Beneath the Sea*. New York: Simon and Schuster, 2001, p. 72.

44. Quoted in Craven, *The Silent War*, p. 72.

45. Quoted in Michael T. Eisenberg, *Shield of the Republic: The United States Navy in an Era of Cold War and Violent*

Peace, 1945–1962. New York: St. Martin's Press, 1993, p. 679.

46. Quoted in Sherry Sontag and Christopher Drew, *Blind Man's Bluff: The Untold Story of American Submarine Espionage:* New York: Public Affairs, 1998, p. 310.

47. Quoted in Eisenberg, *Shield of the Republic,* p. 422.

Chapter 5: Protecting the Homeland

48. Quoted in Peter Pringle and William Arkin, *SIOP: The Secret U.S. Plan for Nuclear War.* New York: W.W. Norton, 1983, p. 133.

49. Quoted in Pringle and Arkin, *SIOP,* p. 134.

50. Quoted in Richard Morenus, *DEW Line: Distant Early Warning, the Miracle of America's First Line of Defense.* New York: Rand McNally, 1957, p. 96.

51. Quoted in Morenus, *DEW Line,* p. 18.

52. Quoted in Douglas T. Miller and Marion Nowak, *The Fifties: The Way We Really Were.* Garden City, NY: Doubleday, 1977, p. 50.

53. Todd Gitlin, *The Sixties: Years of Hope, Days of Rage.* New York: Bantam Books, 1987, p. 22.

54. Quoted in Donald M. Snow, *National Security: Enduring Problems of U.S. Defense Policy.* New York: St. Martin's Press, 1987, p. 182.

55. Deborah Shapley, *Promise and Power: The Life and Times of Robert McNamara.* Boston: Little, Brown, 1993, p. 199.

56. Robert S. McNamara, *Blundering into Disaster: Surviving the First Century of the Nuclear Age.* New York: Pantheon Books, 1986, p. 56.

57. McNamara, *Blundering into Disaster,* p. 57.

58. Quoted in McNamara, *Blundering into Disaster,* p. 57.

59. Quoted in "Strategic Arms Limitation Talks (SALT I)." www.state.gov.

60. Quoted in John Newhouse, *Cold Dawn: The Story of SALT.* New York: Holt, Rinehart, and Winston, 1973, p. 103.

61. Gerard Smith, *Doubletalk: The Story of SALT I.* Garden City, NY: Doubleday, 1980, p. 464.

62. Quoted in Thomas W. Wolfe, *The SALT Experience:* Cambridge, MA: Ballinger, 1979, p. 16.

Chapter 6: Arming Space, Disarming Earth

63. Quoted in Frances FitzGerald, *Way Out There in the Blue: Reagan, Star Wars, and the End of the Cold War.* New York: Simon and Schuster, 2000, p. 20.

64. Quoted in Beth A. Fischer, *The Reagan Reversal: Foreign Policy and the End of the Cold War.* Columbia: University of Missouri Press, 1997, p. 78.

65. Quoted in Philip M. Boffey, William J. Broad, Leslie H. Gelb, Charles Mohr, and Holcomb B. Noble, *Claiming the Heavens: The New York Times Complete Guide to the Star Wars Debate.* New York: Times Books, 1988, pp. 270, 271.

66. Quoted in Fischer, *The Reagan Reversal,* p. 43.

67. Quoted in Fischer, *The Reagan Reversal,* p. 47.

68. Quoted in Strobe Talbott, *The Master of the Game: Paul Nitze and the Nuclear Peace.* New York: Alfred A. Knopf, 1988, p. 285.

69. Quoted in Talbott, *The Master of the Game,* p. 287.

70. Ronald Reagan, *An American Life.* New York: Simon and Schuster, 1990, p. 641.

71. Quoted in Reagan, *An American Life,* p. 677.

72. Reagan, *An American Life,* p. 679.

73. Quoted in Deborah Hart Strober and Gerald S. Strober, *Reagan: The Man and His Presidency.* Boston: Houghton Mifflin, 1998, p. 358.

74. Quoted in Strober and Strober, *Reagan,* pp. 358–59.

75. Quoted in Talbott, *The Master of the Game,* p. 338.

76. Quoted in *Chicago Tribune,* "Bush Officially Withdraws U.S. from 1972 ABM Treaty," June 14, 2002.

★ For Further Reading ★

Books

Christopher Collier and James Lincoln Collier, *The United States in the Cold War: 1945–1989.* New York: Benchmark Books, 2002. An illustrated overview of the Cold War from its beginning to the collapse of communism.

Susan Dudley Gold, *Arms Control.* New York: Twenty-First Century Books, 1997. This book takes a look at the human quest for peace through arms control from the mid-nineteenth century to modern times.

Rebecca Larsen, *Oppenheimer and the Atomic Bomb.* New York: Franklin Watts, 1988. The complete story of the life of the father of the atomic bomb.

David Pietrusza, *The End of the Cold War.* San Diego: Lucent Books, 1995. An overview of communism, how it began, how it affected those who lived under it, and why it finally collapsed.

Richard Smoke, *Think About Nuclear Arms Control.* New York: Walker, 1988. This book follows the arms race from its beginning through the Reagan administration.

L.B. Taylor Jr., *Space: Battleground of the Future?* New York: Franklin Watts, 1988. A brief look at Star Wars and other space-based missile defense systems.

Ann E. Weiss, *The Nuclear Arms Race: Can We Survive It?* Boston: Houghton Mifflin, 1983. Another clearly written account of the nuclear arms race.

Recommended Websites

www.milnet.com. MILNET is a comprehensive website containing information on the organization and strength of military forces worldwide and the weapons used by those forces. Also includes pages on intelligence gathering and terrorism, as well as many links to related sites.

www.fas.org. The website of the Federation of American Scientists contains an exhaustive series of information pages on the development and specifications of just about any nuclear or conventional weapons used by the major powers today. Includes charts and photographs of weapons and information on military analysis, nuclear resources, intelligence, and space policy.

www.astronautix.com. Encyclopedia Astronautica is a comprehensive resource for information on spaceflight and rockets used for both civilian and military purposes. Features a wealth of articles on space and astronautics, plus current news of space-related topics.

www.atomictourist.com. The Bureau of Atomic Tourism contains information on museums and various tourist locations around the United States that played a part in America's development of the atomic bomb. Photographs, directions for visitors, and related links are included.

www.strategic-air-command.com. A nongovernmental website devoted to the history, aircraft, and missiles of the Strategic Air Command.

www.cheyennemountain.af.mil. The official website of the Cheyenne Mountain Command Center, the nerve center for North American Aerospace Defense Command (NORAD), United States Space Command (USSPACECOM), and Air Force Space Command (AFSPC).

www.civildefensemuseum.com. This site is an online museum dedicated to civil defense personnel who worked throughout the Cold War to try to protect the public from nuclear attack. Contains photographs, civil defense artwork, sound files, and virtual tours of various air raid shelters.

www.wpafb.af.mil/museum. The official website of the U.S. Air Force Museum contains information on the development of U.S. air power from the Wright Brothers to the present day.

www.index.ne.jp. The Missile Index is a database of world missile systems, currently providing information on almost three hundred missiles developed by the United States and other countries.

☆ Works Consulted ☆

Books

David A. Anderton, *Strategic Air Command: Two-Thirds of the Triad*. New York: Charles Scribner's Sons, 1976. A detailed account of the early years of the Strategic Air Command.

Stanley A. Blumberg and Louis G. Panos, *Edward Teller: Giant of the Golden Age of Physics*. New York: Charles Scribner's Sons, 1990. A definitive and authoritative biography of the physicist whose influence ran from the A- and H-bombs to the Strategic Defense Initiative.

Philip M. Boffey, William J. Broad, Leslie H. Gelb, Charles Mohr, and Holcomb B. Noble, *Claiming the Heavens: The New York Times Complete Guide to the Star Wars Debate*. New York: Times Books, 1988. A comprehensive analysis of the Star Wars project by a Pulitzer Prize–winning team of *New York Times* journalists.

John L. Chapman, *Atlas: The Story of a Missile*. New York: Harper and Brothers, 1960. The author describes the design, testing, and deployment of America's first ICBM; including some general information on how rockets and spacecraft work.

John Piña Craven, *The Silent War: The Cold War Battle Beneath the Sea*. New York: Simon and Schuster, 2001. The author, a key figure in the Cold War navy, relates his experiences with *Nautilus*, the Polaris missile program, and the U.S.-Soviet cat-and-mouse game under the sea.

Paul Dickson, *Sputnik: The Shock of the Century*. New York: Walker, 2001. A highly readable account of the launching of *Sputnik*, the world's first artificial satellite, and the impact it had around the world, especially on the United States.

Robin Edmunds, *The Big Three: Churchill, Roosevelt, and Stalin in Peace and War*. New York: W.W. Norton, 1991. A complete account of how the three major Allied leaders of World War II came together to ultimately defeat Adolf Hitler.

Michael T. Eisenberg, *Shield of the Republic: The United States Navy in an Era of Cold War and Violent Peace, 1945–1962*. New York: St. Martin's Press, 1993. Volume one of a proposed two-volume set, this book is a comprehensive history of the U.S. Navy from the end of World War II through the Cuban Missile Crisis.

Dwight D. Eisenhower, *The White House Years: Waging Peace, 1956–1961.* Garden City, NY: Doubleday, 1965. The second volume of a two-volume memoir, this book presents Eisenhower's recollections of his second term as president of the United States.

Keith Eubank, *Summit at Tehran: The Untold Story.* New York: William Morrow, 1985. The story of the first wartime summit conference, which began the process for ending World War II and laid the foundation for the future political alignment of Europe.

Faculty Members at the Massachusetts Institute of Technology, *The Nuclear Almanac: Confronting the Atom in War and Peace.* Reading, MA: Addison-Wesley, 1984. A fascinating, though now dated, compendium of articles covering all aspects of nuclear weapons, from the physics of nuclear explosions to radiation and public health.

Beth A. Fischer, *The Reagan Reversal: Foreign Policy and the End of the Cold War.* Columbia: University of Missouri Press, 1997. The author examines Ronald Reagan's change in attitude toward the Soviet Union, from viewing it as an "evil empire" to searching for an understanding between the superpowers.

Frances FitzGerald, *Way Out There in the Blue: Reagan, Star Wars, and the End of the Cold War.* New York: Simon and Schuster, 2000. This Pulitzer Prize–winning author provides a new look at Ronald Reagan, his dream of protecting America with Star Wars, and his role in ending the Cold War.

Lawrence Freedman, *The Evolution of Nuclear Strategy.* New York: St. Martin's Press, 1983. This book presents a comprehensive overview of the various nuclear strategies used, or contemplated being used, throughout the Cold War.

Todd Gitlin, *The Sixties: Years of Hope, Days of Rage.* New York: Bantam Books, 1987. The author documents the turbulent decade of the 1960s, focusing especially on the growth of the youth movement and the political power of the New Left that was behind it.

Leslie R. Groves, *Now It Can Be Told: The Story of the Manhattan Project.* 1962. Reprint: New York: Da Capo Press, 1983. The story of the Manhattan Project by the military officer charged with taking it from uncoordinated groups of scientists spread out across the United States to its ultimately successful conclusion in the skies over Japan.

David Holloway, *Stalin and the Bomb: The Soviet Union and Atomic Energy 1939–1956.* New Haven, CT: Yale University Press, 1994. The story of how the Soviet Union developed its own atomic and hydrogen bombs.

Michael Kort, *The Columbia Guide to the Cold War.* New York: Columbia University Press, 1998. A guide to the Cold War featuring a narrative history, a dictionary of names and terms, a chronology, and a resource list.

William Lanouette, with Bela Silard, *Genius in the Shadows: A Biography of Leo Szilard, the Man Behind the Bomb*. New York: Charles Scribner's Sons, 1992. A definitive biography of the man who developed the idea of atomic weapons, only to work later to outlaw them.

Chuck Lawliss, *The Submarine Book: An Illustrated History of the Attack Submarine*. Short Hills, NJ: Burford Books, 2000. A highly readable account of the submarine from the first crude underwater vessels to the April 2000 sinking of the Russian submarine *Kursk*.

Curtis E. Lemay, *Superfortress: The Story of the B-29 and American Air Power*. New York: McGraw-Hill, 1988. A well-written history of a landmark aircraft by the commander of the Strategic Air Command during the first decade of the Cold War.

Leona Woods Marshall Libby, *The Uranium People*. New York: Crane, Russak, 1979. A personal look at the scientists who made up the Manhattan Project by one of the few female scientists to work on the project.

David McCullough, *Truman*. New York: Touchstone Books, 1992. Pulitzer Prize–winning biography of the president thrust into the position of deciding whether or not to drop the atomic bomb.

Robert S. McNamara, *Blundering into Disaster: Surviving the First Century of the Nuclear Age*. New York: Pantheon Books, 1986. A concise analysis of the dangers of nuclear arms by the man who was secretary of defense for Presidents Kennedy and Johnson.

Douglas T. Miller and Marion Nowak, *The Fifties: The Way We Really Were*. Garden City, NY: Doubleday, 1977. An in-depth cultural and social history of the first full decade of the Cold War.

Richard Morenus, *DEW Line: Distant Early Warning, the Miracle of America's First Line of Defense*. New York: Rand McNally, 1957. A firsthand account of the construction and operation of the DEW Line.

J. Robert Moskin, *Mr. Truman's War*. New York: Random House, 1996. The story of Truman's first five months as president and the decisions he made as he led the United States to victory in World War II and into the Cold War era.

John Newhouse, *Cold Dawn: The Story of SALT*. New York: Holt, Rinehart, and Winston, 1973. An account of the Strategic Arms Limitation Talks drawn from personal conversations by the author with many of the people involved with the talks.

Arnold A. Offner, *Another Such Victory: President Truman and the Cold War, 1945–1953*. Stanford, CA: Stanford University Press, 2002. A thoroughly researched book that reexamines the effectiveness of Truman's Cold War policies.

Dennis Piszkiewicz, *The Nazi Rocketeers: Dreams of Space and Crimes of War*. Westport, CT: Praeger, 1995. The story of how Wernher von Braun and other German rocket scientists went from dreams of space exploration to building weapons of destruction.

Norman Polmar, *Strategic Weapons: An Introduction*. New York: Crane, Russak, 1975. A useful primer by a prolific and well-respected military historian.

Norman Polmar and Thomas B. Allen, *Rickover*. New York: Simon and Schuster, 1982. A comprehensive biography of one of the most controversial men in naval history—Admiral Hyman G. Rickover, the father of the "nuclear navy."

Peter Pringle and William Arkin, *SIOP: The Secret U.S. Plan for Nuclear War*. New York: W.W. Norton, 1983. An in-depth examination of the little-known plan the U.S. military would use to fight a nuclear war.

Ronald Reagan, *An American Life*. New York: Simon and Schuster, 1990. The autobiography of the man who went from small-town Illinois to the White House by way of Hollywood.

Richard Rhodes, *Dark Sun: The Making of the Hydrogen Bomb*. New York: Simon and Schuster, 1995. The story of the development of the world's first thermonuclear weapon.

——, *The Making of the Atomic Bomb*. New York: Simon and Schuster, 1986. A highly readable, comprehensive account of the building of the atomic bomb.

Deborah Shapley, *Promise and Power: The Life and Times of Robert McNamara*. Boston: Little, Brown, 1993. A biography of Robert McNamara, the secretary of defense who served through the crises of missiles in Cuba and war in Vietnam.

John Sharnik, *Inside the Cold War: An Oral History*. New York: Arbor House, 1987. A history of the Cold War that includes reminiscences from diplomats, military leaders, and ordinary people who affected, or were affected by, the Cold War.

Gerard Smith, *Doubletalk: The Story of SALT I*. Garden City, NY: Doubleday, 1980. A complete history of the Strategic Arms Limitation Talks by the chief U.S. negotiator.

Donald M. Snow, *National Security: Enduring Problems of U.S. Defense Policy*. New York: St. Martin's Press, 1987. A study of national security problems that faced the United States during the Cold War.

Sherry Sontag and Christopher Drew, *Blind Man's Bluff: The Untold Story of American Submarine Espionage*. New York: Public Affairs, 1998. A fascinating account of the little-known, extremely dangerous cat-and-mouse games played by U.S. and Soviet submarines.

G. Harry Stine, *ICBM*. New York: Orion Books, 1991. This book, written by a former aerospace engineer, tells the story of how the intercontinental ballistic missile was developed, from the earliest research in Germany to Cold War confrontations.

Deborah Hart Strober and Gerald S. Strober, *Reagan: The Man and His Presidency.* Boston: Houghton Mifflin, 1998. An oral history of the Reagan presidency, based on interviews with more than one hundred of Reagan's contemporaries and associates.

Strobe Talbott, *The Master of the Game: Paul Nitze and the Nuclear Peace.* New York: Alfred A. Knopf, 1988. This behind-the-scenes look at nuclear arms reduction focuses on Paul Nitze, the U.S. defense adviser who helped create the NSC-68 report.

H.G. Wells, *The Last War: A World Set Free.* Lincoln: University of Nebraska Press, 2001. A new printing of Wells's science fiction novel about the effects of an atomic war on society.

Thomas W. Wolfe, *The SALT Experience.* Cambridge, MA: Ballinger, 1979. A complete history of the SALT I and II negotiations.

Periodical

Chicago Tribune, "Bush Officially Withdraws U.S. from 1972 ABM Treaty," June 14, 2002.

Internet Sources

"The Baruch Plan." www.nuclearfiles.org. This site, a project of the Nuclear Age Peace Foundation, has a wealth of information on nuclear arms, nuclear energy, and disarmament.

"History of USS *Thresher* (SSN 593)," *Dictionary of American Naval Fighting Ships,*

Naval Historical Center website. www.history.navy.mil. This website is the Internet link to the official history program of the Department of the Navy, with information on all aspects of U.S. naval history.

Roger D. Launius, "*Sputnik* and the Origins of the Space Age." www.hq.nasa.gov. The website of the National Aeronautics and Space Administration contains the history of space flight, biographies of astronauts, and technical diagrams of U.S. spacecraft.

Gene P. McManus, "BMEWS—510 Full Days—Thule, Top of the World." www.bwcinet.com. A personal essay about life at a BMEWS station during the Cold War.

"On 35th Anniversary of JFK Address, World Still Waits for Nuclear Test Ban." Coalition Issue Brief, vol. 2, no. 15, June 10, 1998. www.clw.org. This website was created by the Council for a Livable World, an organization founded by physicist Leo Szilard. Its purpose is to disseminate information about nuclear arms and arms control.

Stephen I. Schwartz et al., "The 51-Pound Mistake," from "Atomic Audit," *Bulletin of the Atomic Scientists*, September/October 1998. www.bullatomsci.org. This is the publication of the Educational Foundation for Nuclear Science, an organization dedicated to educating citizens about global security and nuclear weapons issues.

"Strategic Arms Limitation Talks (SALT I)." www.state.gov. This is the official website of the U.S. State Department.

"Treaty on Principles Governing the Activities of States in the Exploration and Use of Outer Space, Including the Moon and Other Celestial Bodies." www.state.gov. This is the official U.S. State Department website.

★ Index ★

★ Picture Credits ★

★ About the Author ★

Craig E. Blohm has been writing magazine articles on historical subjects for children for more than fifteen years. He has also written for social studies textbooks and has conducted workshops in writing history for children. A native of Chicago, he has worked for more than twenty-five years in the field of television production as a writer, producer, and director. He is currently the television and radio production coordinator at Purdue University Calumet in Hammond, Indiana. He and his wife, Desiree, live in Tinley Park, Illinois, and have two sons, Eric and Jason.